Every manager should read *iCoach*. Today coaching is a basic management skill like finance or marketing. Every manager must know how to build leaders. No matter where you are in the organization, Dr. Zweifel gives you the essential toolkit for getting the best out of your people.
—**Marshall Goldsmith, Thinkers50 #1 Leadership Thinker in the World**

A punchy book that strips executive coaching back to the essentials. Here's what to do, *and* what not to do, to be effective.
—**Michael Bungay Stanier, author of *WSJ*-bestseller *The Coaching Habit***

The context for leaders has changed fundamentally. You've got more complexity, more innovation and technological change, more opportunities, but also more risks and less trust. In this new context, knowing how to breed not followers but authentic, self-directed leaders around you—people with purpose and psychological stamina who think for themselves—is of utmost importance. *iCoach* shows you how. If you lead anything, use this book to lead your teams to sustainable, and meaningful, high performance.
—**Dr. Daniel Vasella, former Chairman & CEO, Novartis AG**

This is exactly what I wanted to do for a living. Work with people and help them developing as leaders! And this is exactly what I am doing nowadays! Thomas has been a source of inspiration for a profound professional and life change.
—**Elsa Regan-Klapisz, former Danone executive; Executive Coach, Facilitator, Leadership Specialist**

Dr. Zweifel is a man who deserves a title that is all too often bestowed without merit, but in this case is truly deserved: "miracle worker."
—**David Searby, program officer, U.S. State Department**

iCoach offers an effective framework that will guide you to be-

come a better leader and a great coach with impact and success.
—**Ingrid Deltenre, former CEO, Swiss Television SRF; multiple board member**

The book managers have been looking for to improve their leadership and coaching skills: Thomas has written it.
—**Daniel Hager, CEO, Hager Group**

I learned a lot from Thomas' questions and suggestions to land in and fulfill my role as CEO.
—**Willi Heinzelmann, CEO, Cinetrade**

In an increasingly complex and unpredictable world, we need to go beyond traditional management in order to unleash the performance of our teams and generate maximum impact. In *iCoach*, Thomas boils down more than 30 years of world-class coaching experience and gives us invaluable insights on how to boost leadership and performance in our organizations.
—**Géry Gedlek, CIO, Assura SA**

It's not about sheer advice, it's about recognizing how to empower yourself. The approach did provide me with a toolbox so powerful, it will take years to fully unleash its potential. The principles and concepts are pure and lean and will bloom on fertile ground, nourished by a humble disposition of self-reflection. Impressive, impactful and enjoyable!
—**Samuel Kessler, Head HR Policy and HR Risk & Control, Credit Suisse**

I have reached new heights of self-awareness and have developed my leadership skills beyond my personal expectation. Thomas moves the management and leadership theory off the page and into the real world to deliver real results for businesses and individuals.
—**Trevor Isherwood, Executive Director / Head Marketing for Global Emerging Markets, UBS**

Have you ever asked yourself why Roger Federer (any pro for that matter) has a coach and you or your colleagues don't? No worries, you don't need to hire a coach: This superb book will help you bring the very best out of your people and empower them to go beyond themselves—but it works only if *you* are willing to change. *iCoach* leads you along the path, and you're lucky to have Thomas as a mountain guide.
—**Dr. Alexander Herzog, CFO, Regio Energie Solothurn**

Dr. Zweifel gave me essential tools and technology for building my business. We have been growing steadily, we made the INC 500 fastest growing company in America for two years in a row. We are fortunate to have Dr. Zweifel.
—**Richard Zaher, CEO, Paramount Business Jets**

Even if you are not a CEO but a professional seeking insights and guidelines for everyday interactions that boost people's capacities, *iCoach* is a treasure chest—I always find something insightful I can put to good use right away.
—**Dr. Elisabeth Stern, cross-cultural consultant & coach**

Have you heard? "The human being at the center." Finally a book that is honest with you and itself. A transparent, fresh and productive book on enabling people as the key change agents. *iCoach* promises less and delivers more.
—**Willi Helbling, CEO, Business Professionals Network**

iCoach keeps the bold promise in its subtitle: With Dr. Thomas D. Zweifel's simple system, you will free yourself, boost leadership around you, and ultimately make major change. Dr. Zweifel has the perfect feeling and knowledge for empowering people and bringing them closer to their true self and power. Very inspiring and helpful for anyone who wants to go beyond average thinking.
—**Martin Zoller, Author, Producer and Future Analyst**

To produce no-kidding breakthrough results, you need a catalyst—something that will positively disrupt the status quo—and I found *iCoach* to achieve this precisely. Dr. Thomas Zweifel leverages 30+ years of masterful coaching experience to lead you along your journey as a coach, which unquestionably leads to new openings for you and your business.
—**Tanya Privé, Partner at Legacy Transformational Consulting**

Awesome. Every small business with a team environment needs this.
—**Bill Sparks, CEO, Prodox LLC**

The essence of coaching—awareness in myself—manifested itself. I wish I had had your tools 35 years ago when I was starting out.
—**Werner Brandmayr, former President, ConocoPhillips Europe**

I learned that I could coach superiors, not only subordinates. I can convince superiors to do things they would not have done without my persistence.
—**Steve Miley, Executive Vice President, Cemex**

While we did not achieve our breakthrough goal of 16% growth, we did produce 11%, at a time when the industry experienced negative growth. And in the process of producing these results, we began spreading the coaching philosophy in the organization. I see new possibilities, but also pathways for action.
—**Michael Gentz, Managing Director, ConocoPhillips Germany**

Great book, I loved it! Exactly what's missing in the agile industry. *iCoach* is the framework, toolkit and step-by-step guide for anyone involved in agile methodologies like scrum or holacracy. The book focuses on a key aspect, the cornerstone for anyone who wants to achieve great performance without force:

the coach him- or herself. *iCoach* provides everything you need to start coaching right away.
—**Philippe Baeriswyl, Partner, Eiriz Groupe SA**

The team is relating to me differently. They are pushing for answers and working together. I feel like a person and not a boss. Thank you.
—**Lawrence Obstfeld, CEO, Image Navigation**

A really interesting book that targets different aspects of leadership—from the foundation of coaching to explaining how things really get done in the leadership world. *iCoach* is useful for everyone—leader or not—the insights not only help you in your business but also in your private life.
—**Tamara Bürkli, Strategic Assistant to the CEO bei Similasan AG**

iCoach presents concise and pragmatic guidelines that help balancing and transitioning between manager, advisor and coaching roles. But Thomas Zweifel goes far beyond that: He provides a thought-provoking framework on how to inspire and encourage leaders who are creating and shaping the future (of organizations).
—**Dr. Erich Greiner, CEO, Cedrus Therapeutics Inc.**

A personal growth experience that will equip you with the mindset to perform in the 21st century, when "human skills" or "EQ" are becoming increasingly important success factors.
—**Gabin Meier, Head of Strategy & Business Development, Jax Coco**

I find Dr. Zweifel's work to be a powerful complement and source of excellent insights into the actual drivers of organizational performance.
—**Chalmers Brothers, Author,** *Language and the Pursuit of Happiness*, **TED Speaker "How Language Generates Your World and Mine"**

Dr. Thomas Zweifel's thinking out of the box and in terms of breakthroughs helped to grow my company into a new dimension of trust, team spirit and results.
—**Dylan Watts, CEO, Jaro Fruit**

Timely and relevant. A fantastic book by Thomas Zweifel, full of practical insights, addressing the important issue of producing extraordinary results through others.
—**Vip Vyas, CEO, Distinctive Performance Ltd; INSEAD Knowledge Contributor**

Although I have 25 years experience in managing people, *iCoach* gave me vital insights into the mystery of pulling for people's peak performance, as well as a practical system for empowerment. A must-read.
—**Dr. Felix Obrist, CEO and Member of the Board, Nahrin AG**

iCoach

The Simple Little Formula for Freeing Yourself, Boosting People Power, and Changing the World

By Dr. Thomas D. Zweifel

©2019 Thomas D. Zweifel
All rights reserved, including the right of reproduction in whole or in part in any form.

Dr. Thomas D. Zweifel

Copyright ©2019 by Thomas D. Zweifel

This edition published by iHorizon.

All rights reserved. Published in the United States of America. No part of this book may be used or reproduced in any manner whatsoever without the written permission of the publisher.

ISBN 978-1-68749-294-4

Zweifel, Thomas D., 1962-
 iCoach 1: coach hat: the simple little formula for freeing yourself, boosting people power, and changing the world / Thomas D. Zweifel—1st ed.

Includes bibliographical references.

1. Leadership. 2. Executive Coaching.

Manufactured in the United States of America 10 9 8 7 6 5 4 3 2 1

*"As for the best leaders, the people do not notice their existence.
The next best leaders, the people admire.
The next, the people fear, and the next the people hate.
But when the best leader's work is done,
the people say, "We did it ourselves".*
—Lao Tzu, 6th century BCE

Dr. Thomas D. Zweifel

Dedication

To Gabrielle, Tina and Hannah
who test my leadership
and deepen my humanity
every day

TABLE OF CONTENTS

Why—and How—Use *iCoach*? (Don't Skip This.)
Acknowledgments
Chapter 1. What Do You Want to Escape? And What Is Success?
Chapter 2. What Coaching is *Not*
Chapter 3. Sparring Partner: What's the Difference?
Chapter 4. Distinction: What Coaching *Is*
Chapter 5. Cat-and-Mouse: Catching Coaching Opportunities
Chapter 6. Quick Win I: Get a Player (= Client)
Chapter 7. Mind Shift: Life As Conversations
Chapter 8. Framework: Five Steps to Power & Impact
Chapter 9. Six Key Coaching Questions
Chapter 10. Exit Strategy: Fire Yourself
Chapter 11. Sustainability—7 Debrief Questions
Chapter 12. Quick Win III: Making Money as a Coach (If You Want)
What Are You Gonna Do About It? Getting Into Action
The Road to Mastery: The *iCoach* Series
Further Readings
The Author
Other Books by Thomas D. Zweifel
ThomasZweifel.com Processes
Notes

Dr. Thomas D. Zweifel

Why—and How—Use *iCoach*? (Don't Skip This.)

*I have no theory. I only show something. I show reality…
I take those who listen to me by the hand and lead them to the window.
I push open the window and point outside.—
I have no theory, but I lead a conversation.*
—Martin Buber

In a recent executive coaching session, a senior manager at a global bank told me: "I have been a player and a manager. I want to be a player-coach." He was a top performer. As a player, he had scored key goals; as a manager, he now prepared a big unit—some 120 people—for scoring the goals. (In fact his shop produced 2.5%, one-fortieth, of the entire bank's revenue worldwide, which was some $32 billion annually.) But there were limits to his performance. As a player-coach, he could lead leaders and cause a breakthrough in his and his team's impact.

The key word is *impact.* If you want to be a player-coach and boost leadership and performance around you—while earning the respect of direct reports, peers and bosses as a guru—*iCoach* is for you. Just like my client, you may want (or need) to boost your impact. But you've reached the limit of your capacity. Perhaps you—like countless others—suffer from the famous Peter Principle: The very expertise that got you where you are today is no longer enough for tackling the leadership challenges before you now. Your organization offers some performance incentives, but they fall short of inspiring sorely needed innovations. At times you, like others, feel the need to use force, power plays or temper tantrums to get your way. You seem to be flying blind: People are a mystery and their performance volatile and unpredictable, like a lottery. People are unreliable or at least a pain in the neck. You enjoy some measure of authority, but sometimes it feels like you're merely a cog in a wheel, powerless, at the effect of forces you cannot control. In the worst case, the organizational culture around you is one of lies, CYA (cover-your-ass), pretense, or even cheating.

As long as one (or several) of these statements applies

to your situation, then this book is for you. I make available to you, and to as many leaders as possible, the secrets it took me over three decades to master: how to coach someone, anyone, to unleash their true essence, be at their best, and realize their vision. And since today we all must be leaders—leaders of our lives in an uncertain world and under a plethora of choices, leaders of our children, our colleagues, our companies, our communities and ultimately of our legacy to future generations— that means anyone.

In the 21st century, more and more humans are free to shape their own lives. The Internet, globalization and flattened organizational hierarchies allow each of us to impact our organizations and societies. In this new environment, we can no longer rely on our elected leaders or captains of industry—the Wise Men—alone to provide leadership. Each of us must lead, and we must be armed with the right tools to do so.

Over a decade ago, Harvard professor John P. Kotter declared: "My vision is to create 100 million new leaders. That's not 100 million CEOs, nor is it something that can be achieved next year. But it is a question of enabling many, many more people to provide leadership in their jobs — no matter what their jobs are."[1] This book stands on the shoulders of the management guru's inspiring words. And why stop at 100 million? How about a *billion* leaders—leaders of their lives, their families, their companies, communities, societies?

Leadership is like fire, or the Internet: It's not good or bad in and of itself, it's simply a tool for making something happen. I am convinced that leadership is *the* critical element missing for bringing about the future we want—be it innovation or change, tackling transnational issues like migration or terrorism, or boosting performance and sustainable growth. I am convinced that the key ingredient to performance is not primarily technology, but people. And I am equally convinced that coaching, done right, is *the* indispensable (and most cost-effective) process for harnessing and unleashing leadership if organizations are not only to survive but prosper in the 21st century. Let me tell you how I arrived at this conviction.

An Unusual Coaching Education
It may be strange to hear this from someone at the top of his game, whose clients have produced "hard" results measured in the billions while rising to C-level positions or advancing their careers (or, in the case of some, quitting their companies and moving on to build their own enterprise or do what they truly love), let alone "soft" and intangible results like self-awareness, trust, credibility, communication, alignment, inspiration, or teamwork, but: I never had a formal coaching education. I learned coaching in the most circuitous way. That is how life works, at least my life. In fact, looking back, my experience as an actor and director at Theater Basel and Werktheater Basel, from age seventeen to twenty-two, taught me invaluable skills that I came to recognize decades later as essential to leadership and coaching. It's hardly accidental that the word "performance" is a term used in both business and the performing arts.

Harvard professor Sharon Daloz Parks observed that although "The phrase 'the art of leadership' is certainly well worn," she went on to suggest "that art, artist and artistry be given a more prominent place within the lexicon of leadership theory and practice."[2] I couldn't agree more. The skillset I learned at the start of my professional career in theater and film ranges from empathy—putting myself into the skin of any character, whether it was a suicidal student or a callous surgeon—to self-regulation of my emotions, from mimics to body language, from public speaking to being myself on stage while being watched by hundreds (and later, via TV camera, by millions) of people.

Perhaps most importantly, I learned the art of improvisation—giving up control under uncertainty in a dynamic, interdependent environment, yet single-mindedly pursuing an objective and never losing sight of the play's or movie's bigger story. This skillset later became a key asset in the face of all kinds of business challenges, not least dynamic strategy and executive coaching. The leadership expert and Harvard professor Ronald Heifetz has shown how

> acts of leadership require the ability to walk the razor's edge without getting your feet too cut up—working that edge place between known problems and unknown solutions, between popularity and anxious hostility. Artistic leadership is able to remain curious and creative in the complexity and chaos of swamp issues, often against the odds. As we have seen, those who practice adaptive leadership must confront, disappoint, and dismantle and at the same time energize, inspire, and empower."[3]

The operative word in Heifetz's description is the last one, *empower*. Linda St. Clair, a senior manager at a technology company who, like me, learned much about the art of coaching in the theater, recalled: "By the time dress rehearsal arrives, the director has given the work away, becoming an observer, taking notes, but talking about it later—becoming less 'a director' and more a coach, guide, mentor, companion, ally."[4]

Then my life took yet another turn: I became a manager. Over three decades ago, in 1986, when the word "coaching" barely existed outside of sports, my boss at the time—the organization's president—thrust me into a global leadership role, in charge of performance management in 27 global affiliates who reported to me—nominally. In actuality, they were not at all required to listen, let alone obey. In a legal sense they were not accountable to me, but to their respective national boards of directors, their real legal and fiduciary bosses. So I could never tell any global affiliate what to do. I was "forced" to inspire them, persuade them, listen to them. Despite my grand title as Director of Global Operations, I had virtually no authority over them; I couldn't hire or fire people in Japan, or determine the expense budget in Sweden. I could not force my colleagues to do anything they didn't want to do. My direct reports were not on my payroll, so I couldn't even offer them bonuses or other performance incentives.

Instead of managing by control, I learned to lead through

inspiration, alignment, empowerment, mobilization, and yes, sometimes manipulation (always for the greater good of course). The organization's mission—to bring about the end of world hunger—was so outlandish that its managers had to unleash leaders at all levels, from heads of state like Nelson Mandela of South Africa or Abdou Diouf of Senegal, to women Panchayat (district) leaders across India, to over 65,000 volunteer animators in Bangladesh. We still had to meet the organization's business imperatives. And my objectives outstripped my resources—they were far bigger than what I could accomplish with the existing people capacity, so I was constantly forced to inspire people to rise above themselves and take action along the overall strategy. This was true for all managers at the organization, since our job was to create a global movement to carry out our mission. The organization's motto "unleashing the human spirit" went much deeper than a mere slogan: The ratio of staff to activists was extraordinary—some 150 staff worldwide in charge of coaching and mobilizing close to 100,000 activists. Our relationships were not transactional. Volunteers had no contracts—if they didn't want their jobs anymore, they would simply walk away. So old top-down management techniques were futile.

Only in hindsight did I see that my coaching—coupled with constant efforts to maintain global alignment and management by objectives—had produced the results: From 1992 to 1996 we increased revenue by 45% each year—annually compounded—while holding expenses stable, and empowered millions of people to rise up and take charge of their lives and communities. That is what coaching is all about. Quite frankly, it was a pain in the neck at the time, but in hindsight it was far and away the best performance coaching school I could have asked for.

In 1996, I left the organization—and was immediately pursued by several consulting companies. But I soon realized that I had lost the appetite for being in somebody else's show. In 1997 I became CEO of Swiss Consulting Group and built it into a boutique company with three dozen coaches in twelve countries (I bought out my partner a year later and ended up selling the company in 2013). Over the years my colleagues and I coached hundreds of top and senior managers as well as entrepreneurs to rise above themselves and produce results previously considered impossible.

With the late management theorist and consultant Peter Drucker, I assert that all organizations, from firms to governments, from churches to the military, face essentially the same challenges: to meet organizational objectives through people. Throughout this time, I have applied the same principles of coaching to our clients in all sectors—corporate, government, military, nonprofit, for-benefit—and my clients have invariably used the coaching methods in this book to produce breakthrough results. So it is time to make available the tools I have developed from working with CEOs and C-level executives, heads of state like Nelson Mandela, Nobel laureates like Amartya Sen, but also from untold leaders in India or Haiti.

How to Use This Book: Rule #1—Doubt
My last name "Zweifel" is German for "doubt" or "skepticism." You may be wondering why someone named "Doubt," or worse, "Doubting Thomas," would write leadership books, since leaders are supposed to brim with confidence. (Why my late parents called me Thomas, in addition to Zweifel, is beyond me. Well, perhaps it's like in math, where minus and minus equals plus, so doubting doubt equals faith? But that's another story.) On the contrary, in my view an integral element of leadership is to doubt, question, be skeptical, and not accept things at face value. I am in good company with this view. Already Voltaire said that "Doubt is not a pleasant condition, but certainty is absurd."[5] The Spanish philosopher George Santayana wrote centuries later that

> Skepticism is the chastity of the intellect and it is shameful to surrender it too soon or to the first comer; there is nobility in preserving it coolly and proudly through long youth, until at last, in the ripeness of instinct and discretion, it can be

safely exchanged for fidelity and happiness.[6]

To the nuclear physicist and Nobel laureate Richard Feynman, doubt was indispensable for innovation. Believe me, I am not saying this lightly. Perhaps the defining moment in my life, above all others, was the premature death of my younger sister at the age of eighteen from a heroin overdose. This premature, fundamental and unjust loss led me to doubt not only the meaning of my own life, but of life itself. How could life allow for such needless suffering—not to speak of untold hunger, war and disease?

At the same time, this existential doubt allowed me to reach rock bottom. I understood that in a world of such senseless death, life is not inherently meaningful. It is inherently meaningless. And on that foundation of nothing, I could give life the meaning I chose—I could either fall into the abyss my sister had fallen into; or I could invent a meaning greater than myself. Without boring you with the story, I chose the latter. I resolved to make my life mean something, to be a leader who moves the needle.

Perhaps leadership is based on being ridden by doubts and acting nevertheless, much as expressed by the composer Arnold Schönberg, who famously held that courage is not the absence of fear, but action *with or despite* fear.

Speaking of doubts, let me plant some right here. My **Ground Rule #1**: If you think that this book is a guarantee to make something happen, you are wrong. Books rarely accomplish anything. People do, and they may or may not accomplish things from reading a book. This book—any book—can at best give some insights, a framework for thinking before, between and after your actions. If you want this book to be useful to you, go out into the market, into the battlefield, and actually live life. It works best if you approach the book with a specific project, relationship, or venture in mind. As my doctoral advisor Adam Przeworski liked to say, "Theories are not to be believed —theories are to be used." If you don't apply the tools in this book, it might be interesting, instructive, clever, but it will remain theoretical—it will not truly affect things.

In my leadership courses, I ask the students at the start of each semester to come up with a 100-day leadership objective that is a real stretch—unpredictable, visionary, but also measurable and concrete. Many of them are highly original. One of my Columbia students wanted to build an executive jet company; another launched a Brazilian restaurant in Harlem; another created a development project for children in his native Rwanda. Over the years, more than 2,500 students —and hundreds of managers and teams in Fortune 500 firms, governments, and UN agencies—have designed and carried out such pilot projects to jumpstart their futures. The results have been nothing short of staggering. One former Columbia student called me ten years later to say that the executive jet company he founded in the leadership class was now on *Inc.* magazine's list of the 500 fastest-growing companies. A coaching client produced €5 million in sales from innovative products not on the market when he started his pilot. In 2015, one student raised $10 million for his innovative sportswear company. This is what I live for (in addition to being a family man of course) —having conversations with leaders that have them shift their dreams into possibilities, make those possibilities doable, and then achieve them.

I cannot guarantee that you will have the same results— that very much depends on your actions—but I am asking you to do likewise. Take a few minutes right now and think of something you really want—an objective that is larger than you, that you cannot achieve alone, that requires you to coach others.

- ☐ What objective is so vast that it would stretch you way beyond who you are today and would require you to pull for the best in others? (Tip: include many people in your objective.)
- ☐ Who around you (colleagues, alliance partners, suppliers etc.) would have to be at their best in order to

achieve this objective?
- ☐ What's missing in your leadership to meet this objective? What blockages will you need to transcend? What recurring, chronic issue (or opportunity) do you face, for example vis-à-vis colleagues, customers or suppliers (or family members)?

Readers often skip over these types of labs. But perhaps you find it in yourself to grab a pencil and piece of paper—or open the Notes app (or Google Keep, whatever works for you) on your smartphone—and invest a few minutes in answering these questions. What you write down will likely matter at least as much for your ROI as whatever else you read in the book. What if this small investment of your time led you to a new future?

People I work with often start with an objective that involves only themselves, for example wanting to land their dream job or become the CEO of their company. There is nothing wrong with an objective like that. Even so, to achieve such an objective, you would want to add value to the company, lead others to achieving a shared aspiration, and make a mark that qualifies you in the eyes of your colleagues to lead the company. Mary Kay Ash, the founder of Mary Kay Cosmetics, boasted of making more women rich than any other company.[7] Set an objective that is larger than yourself, that "forces" you to coach others to excellence.

Rule #2—Experiment

This leads us to my *Ground Rule #2*: Your work with this book will be only as powerful as your willingness to surrender to the book. One basic rule for coaches is that we don't coach someone unless they're open to coaching. Even if it were possible to coach without a demand for coaching—to force your solution or advice on the other person—the results would be limited or nil, and it would certainly not be fun for either person involved (except for sado-masochists). So whenever you ignore things the book asks of you and you don't work through them, the integrated nature of the book will be lost and you might not gain the benefits available. (So at the risk of being a pest, if you did skip the questions on the previous page, go back now and answer them.)

Ask yourself whether you're willing to try the ideas in this book without nagging or judgment. Our brains are conditioned to knee-jerk reactions like "This is good/bad" or "I like/dislike this." Such super-quick judgments can be useful for dangerous situations, as when you meet a stranger in a dark back alley at 2am, but they are counterproductive for explorations and experiments that lead to real learning. Can you simply do whatever the book asks you to do? After you have worked through the assignments in the book, you will have complete freedom to throw some (or all) of them out. But first try them. Open yourself to the possibility that they might be useful.

Rule #3—Use for Good
Did you know that typical politicians spend up to 90 percent of their time preventing others from unseating them, and as little as 10 percent working for the social good they have been elected to serve? And based on over three decades working with C-level executives, I can safely say that a similar percentage plays out in large businesses (and even small ones), where managers are constantly looking over their shoulder and trust is a scarce commodity.

Therefore, *Ground Rule #3*: Do not use this book for harmful purposes. It offers powerful tools that can be used for building up, as well as destroying, things or people. Ask yourself whether your undertaking, your leadership and your coaching will uplift people in some way. Unless you have that intention (or at least unless that intention is part of your endeavor), rethink your plans before continuing. Too many misguided leaders have done too much harm. All too often, leaders have abused their power to cause damage. If you have any plans to continue this tradition, I ask you to give the book to someone else. As Gandhi said over 50 years ago, "Ask yourself whether the deed you contemplate will be of any use to someone. In other words, will it free the millions of people from poverty..."

Since you're still reading, I will assume from now on that you have good intentions. As my working assumption, all acts can be looked at as performed out of necessity. I believe that all people are driven to whatever they do either by love or by fear. It is clear to me that an assumption of benevolence is more often than not inaccurate, even naïve; but if I did not assume this, I would be unable to write this, or any, book. The question is: At the end of your life, what will you—and others—say about your life, your legacy? What will be written on your tombstone? Will you—and those who come after you—look back upon a life of going through the motions, even damaging people or things, or upon a life of meaning, service and contribution?

The Mystery of Coaching
Although I teach leadership, let me assure you that leadership —including coaching leaders—is an art, not a science (just don't tell Columbia or St. Gallen University I said that). Perhaps leadership is akin to love: We know unequivocally whether it is present or absent, and yet it is hard to describe.

Suppose someone asks you: How long is the coast of England? You might say 2,000 miles, and would be close to accurate. But this answer is only true at a level of extraordinary simplification. The closer we come to the coast of England, the more we have to take into account all the circumferences of all the little pebbles. If we go even closer, we have to measure the circumferences of grains of sand. At the microscopic level, we are shocked to discover that the answer is that the coast of England is— infinite. Perhaps leadership too is like fractals: The closer we look, the more confusing and the less defined it appears.

Despite these paradoxes, or maybe because of them, I trust this book series will provide you with concrete tools you can use in your own quest for leadership.

TDZ
Zurich
September 2019

ACKNOWLEDGMENTS

*I can't understand why people are frightened of new ideas.
I'm frightened of old ones.*
—John Cage

Above all, I am grateful for the life I get to lead. (Believe me, it was not always thus. I was not fed with a silver spoon—I worked hard and at times fought tooth and nail to get where I am today.) The fact that I have lived for more than half a century, and never once faced war, poverty or disease, fills me with deep gratitude. This unprecedented period of peace and wellbeing in our time, at least in most parts of most industrialized countries, should never be taken for granted. And in my view *noblesse oblige*—this privilege gives us the responsibility to rise beyond ourselves and accomplish something greater.

My gratitude is only deepened by everything I have achieved and received—a beautiful and loving family, wealth and financial freedom, impact in the world and powerful leverage through the methodology I was able to develop with the guidance, assistance and yes, coaching by many others. I am grateful to so many people who directly or indirectly, knowingly or not, contributed to who I am and what I do, and therefore to this book. Here are only a few outstanding examples:

The people who mentored me in the art and science of coaching way back in the mid-1980s—before "coaching" was even a business term—and gave me a commitment larger than myself, as well as a global playing field: Joan Holmes, Jay Greenspan, Lawrence Flynn, Linda Howard and Lynne Twist. They practiced what we call "tough love": They each challenged me to go to the edge, to rise beyond what I thought possible for a

iCoach

human being and to cause breakthroughs in performance, but they did not forget empathy and compassion.

Well, almost always. I'll never forget how Jay Greenspan threatened to fire me unless I delivered on my campaign promise of 5 million people enrolled in the organization. And I'll never forget how Lawrence Flynn and I co-led a leadership workshop in the Netherlands, and I said something that I've since forgotten; after I'd finished, he simply told the participants to ignore what I had just said, since it was utterly irrelevant. As I said, it was tough love. That is the essence of performance coaching.

My former student and now business partner, confidant and comrade-in-arms Philippe Baeriswyl, who provides the platforms to turn my crazy ideas into products and bring them to market—and who came up with the idea for this book. My debt of gratitude to Philippe is beyond words.

My former colleagues at Swiss Consulting Group, Insigniam® and Manres AG, who work on the cutting edge of unleashing the human spirit in organizations.

My clients—CEOs and/or senior managers at forty Fortune 500 companies, from Airbus to Zurich Insurance; the prime minister and cabinet of Kazakhstan, the UN Development Programme, the government and civil society of Haiti, the Swiss Federal Office of Health and the U.S. State Department; the U.S. Military Academy at West Point and the U.S. Air Force Academy; and not least a German soccer club—who demonstrate the impact of the coaching approach in their work and results, and provided many of the cases and stories in this book (of course anonymously or with their names changed).

The participants in my keynotes and workshops (I remember fondly the Coach-the-Coaches days at BPN, Cemex or ERNE AG) who experimented with, tested in the action, challenged and helped me refine my concepts; and my 2,500+ leadership students (so far) at Columbia University, St. Gallen University, and other universities in Australia, Israel, Switzerland and the United States, who leverage coaching to breed leaders and boost sustainable growth.

The sages of the ages, particularly the two Martins—Martin Buber, who brought the principles of *I and Thou* and dialogue into the modern discourse and shaped my outlook on life, and Martin Heidegger, who coined the famous phrase "Language is the house of being" and showed me the awesome power of language to build reality (just as the Hebrew word for "word," *davar*, means also "thing").

My agent Christian Dittus, who could well be called my literary coach, who is always supportive of my wild ideas—while not shying away from giving brutally honest feedback on what works and what doesn't—and helps channel them into publishable and value-adding products.

My late parents Dr. Eva Wicki-Schönberg and Dr. Heinz Wicki, who believed in me and later became my first coaching clients (non-paying of course—memorably, we once co-created an inspiring future on my father's seventieth birthday when he told me he had wasted his life and all he wanted was to give up); and finally the people I spend the most time with, my three strong women Gabrielle, Tina and Hannah, who stand by me, give me life and a future to live for, and challenge my coaching concepts pretty much on a daily basis. (Just because I write books on the topic does not mean I never fail—quite the contrary, as you will see.)

Of course all errors and stupidities are mine and mine alone.

CHAPTER 1. WHAT DO YOU WANT TO ESCAPE? AND WHAT IS SUCCESS?

There are many who can execute and display magnificent fireworks; but who knows how to kindle a spark in the darkness of the soul?
—Abraham J. Heschel[8]

Let me begin with a promise. In *iCoach*, I give you the tools that have taken me close to forty years to develop and that I have used in my own life, with clients, business, family and friends. At the risk of sounding boastful, which is quite un-Swiss, I dare say I succeeded beyond my wildest dreams and am deeply grateful for that.

I have built financial freedom and don't have to work anymore (more accurately, work on what I love). I have published eight books, two of which award-winners. I get to teach at Columbia and St. Gallen University, coaching more than 2,500 students (and counting) to build success. I built a company that I sold in 2013, which was not huge (28 people) but quite successful in adding value for its clients (over $9 billion in profits). I had the opportunity to work with presidents and prime ministers, with CEOs and senior managers, with Nobel laureates and with people in the slums of India and Haiti. The tools I have poured into this book have worked for me and my clients (although, to repeat, there is no guarantee they will work for you and yours).

Escape from What?
What do you want to escape? What is the problem this book could solve for you? Let me guess: You might be caught in a situation or structure where nobody listens to you. Or if people do listen, they don't act on your advice or ideas. Your impact might be limited. You might feel like a cog in a wheel.

Maybe you were newly hired as a team leader and were promoted for your technical, marketing, or financial skills (or whatever skills you have). But now you suddenly command a team of people, and you don't know how to do it.

How can you get the best out of these people? Not just through incentives because you pay them a salary, give them perks or bonuses, but in an intrinsic way, mobilizing people through empowerment and coaching. I have seen so many people that arrived at the limit of their capacity. It's the famous Peter Principle where you rise up to the level where you reveal your incompetence. You might have reached a certain degree of incompetence in mobilizing people for action and results.

If you find yourself in one, or several, of these situations, at least some of the time, then you are in the right place.

What Would Success Look Like?
This leads us directly to what is feasible from reading the book —although I must tell you right now: This will not happen by itself. It is not a silver bullet or magical pill that you eat and then you are a master coach. First you must read the book, do the exercises and practice in the action. I will show you every single step along the way, but you have to do those steps. It doesn't happen by itself, and there cannot be any guarantee. Having said that, the opportunity the book affords is that after reading it and applying it, you will have wide and deep impact around you. You will have high-performing people around you. And this need not happen with subordinates only, but also with peers who are on the same level as you and with bosses above

you, because the great advantage of coaching is that you can do it in all directions. It doesn't happen only downward in the hierarchy. It also happens upward or sideways.

You will strengthen people's self-confidence and leadership so they can operate independently and not be reliant upon you, but still be aligned with the strategy of the company or what you want them to do. And since people will be less dependent on you, you will have more freedom, more peace of mind, ease, and grace. You will have power and control over your life, being less determined by other people's agendas and more self-determined.

The Road to Freedom, Power (Impact) and Peace of Mind
Basically, you can get people to do whatever you set your mind to. I call that real power, and it's not power as in forcing someone to do something; that is the old way. The new way is power by giving people power. You will have more power. That may sound kind of mysterious to you right now, but you will see that there is a systematic way of boosting your power from empowering others. "Who is honored?" asks *Ethics of the Fathers*, a compilation of sayings of 2nd-century rabbis. "He who honors others."[9] Ultimately, you will be almost like a guru, the go-to person, the one that provides people power, that is a source of power.

By the way, you may be somebody who doesn't particularly like to work with people. It's not politically correct to say this, but here is the ugly truth: For many if not most of us, working with people is often a royal pain in the neck. It is unpredictable. People have their own agendas and their minds and their moods. If you and I could make things happen just by clicking a mouse or hiring a robot, we would probably prefer that over the tedious work of building alignment, cajoling people into setting goals and doing whatever you want or need them to do, and finally policing their performance and/or compliance. This book will show how you can develop real power in working with other people. Rather than a pain in the neck, co-leading and collaborating could even become something that is enjoyable.

Most organizations, even small businesses, can be places of slavery where you do a lot of things you don't really want to do. Whether it's a large corporation or a small company, an NGO or the military, you are in essence making a deal with the organization: "I give life, a substantial part of my life, for example eight waking hours or more every day, in return for security." Depending on the deal, some of us even give their soul.

Let us recall a principle that is often overlooked: The only reason for building organizations in the first place, and hence for working in an organization, is to have greater impact. That is an opportunity this book offers: that you will have greater impact even while working in an organization. I hope you will have a lot more fun too—that comes with the freedom and with the peace of mind.

Harvard tells us that you can manage up to seven people effectively. Really, in my own management experience, the ideal number of people to manage would be five people. The number of people you can coach is not unlimited, of course, but much greater than five or seven. At any given moment, I coach up to twenty different clients. My consulting business is very selective. I don't take every client, but the ones that offer the highest leverage. It is my privilege not to have to work for money anymore, so I can afford to choose. Enough about me, though: The great thing about coaching is that you can coach a lot more people than you could manage, and that boosts the impact you can have. Call me biased, but: Coaching is the solution. Coaching is the best, highest leverage, most cost-effective investment you can make in your own future as a leader and in the future of your organization. Why? Because you are basically having conversations and the impact, the radius of influence you can have from coaching is so much more than from anything else. And *iCoach* is about how to learn that.

But now, before we jump into coaching, we must step

back for a moment. We must clearly distinguish coaching from other activities. Especially today, so many people call themselves coaches, so many definitions of coaching are bandied about, and so much poses for coaching that is not in fact coaching, that we need to distinguish clearly what coaching is *not*.

CHAPTER 2. WHAT COACHING IS NOT

*Power corrupts,
and absolute power corrupts absolutely.*
—Lord Acton

Katinka Hosszu, the world-class Hungarian swimmer who won three gold medals at the 2016 Rio Olympic Games, has a coach who is also her husband. Over the years, Shane Tusup has pushed Hosszu to stretch her limits, producing six world championship medals, including four golds, two female swimmer of the year awards, and a world record. Hosszu also became the first swimmer ever to surpass $1 million in World Cup series prize money for individual races and overall finishes.[10]

We have seen this mixing of personal and coaching relationships between coaches and athletes in other sports too, most notably in tennis when fathers oversaw the careers of their children. More rare is the coach who is also the athlete's husband.

A core principle of coaching is that the coach should have the freedom to be and do whatever it takes to enable the player's success. But this coach-husband tandem took the principle to an extreme. Tusup is more temperamental than Hosszu, and his eruptions on the pool deck elicited stares, complaints and calls for his removal.

At a 2015 meet of Swimmers from the United States and Europe, the American Josh Prenot tweeted an eight-second video of Tusup throwing an object to the ground and kicking the banner board that ran the length of the pool after Hosszu's loss to Missy Franklin in the 200 meter freestyle.

"I've seen a lot of inappropriate and not-O.K. behavior in Shane," said Jessica Hardy, an Olympic medalist who used to train with Hosszu. "I've seen coaches exhibit that kind of behavior in training, but this is another level. It's scary." Dave Salo, who coached Hosszu until shortly after the 2012 Olympics, worried that "the biggest issue with her is her husband. I think you have to look at her motivation. Is it fear or confidence that is driving her?"[11]

Hosszu and Tusup admitted that theirs is a complicated relationship, but both insist that it is not unhealthy. "I get a bad rep in the U.S." Tusup said, "because these parents in the stands, they're going, 'He's such a jerk; he yells at her when she doesn't swim fast.' No, the hard part of swimming is that there's a lot of times you just settle for O.K. and we agreed that the goal was never to settle for O.K., that we're going to keep pushing, even if we don't get it, to be great, to be amazing, to be legendary."

You might say the end justifies the means. And in sports, this kind of coaching might push athletes to go beyond what they think is possible. But in my view this is not coaching. This is brute force that might yield immediate results but will not be sustainable and may lead to over-dependence of the player on the coach. The work of the coach is to lead the player to self-determination, to independence, and to finding his or her own solution. But I'm getting ahead of myself. What is coaching that deserves the name?

In order to answer that, we need to first ask what coaching is *not*. When I started coaching in the 1980s, the term "coaching" barely existed outside of sports. Today there are thousands of books and articles on coaching. The majority still focuses on athletic performance.[12] A second group is on external coaches who provide either performance management or psychological counseling in organizations. Many articles in this field emphasize the need to tune into the psychological world of the client.[13] A third group covers the role of the executive as coach for subordinates. These articles suggest that managers who don't know how to coach effectively will suffer from poor organizational performance and stunted career opportunities.[14]

But there are problems with the existing literature. One, the books on coaching that appeared in the last decade are all based on a very small sample: little over a dozen recent empirical studies.[15] Two, much of the work on coaching consists of exhortation and tips. There is a dearth of empirical research on the actual work of senior practitioners in the field. Yes, there are empirical studies: for example, several studies demonstrated management skill improvements as a function of coaching programs. One study reported on a program that successfully improved the performance of salespeople whose supervisors became better coaches. Another showed improved note-taking and charting by hospital staff who had been coached effectively. Yet another showed that supervisors who trained in coaching and handling employee complaints improved employee retention.[16] But how do you do it? And, crucially: How do you *not* do it?

Coaching vs. Forcing
The number one distinction is that coaching is never pushing. If you are committed to something and advocate that people commit to the same thing, that is not coaching—it is forcing. You really must make sure the client or the other person you are talking to is at least as committed as you are to their result. More than being committed to the result, you must be committed to the person's *success*, which includes their growth and their productivity. But you are not accountable for the result; the other person is accountable for the result.

Let's draw an analogy. Ivan Ljubičić coaches Roger Federer, at least as of this writing. Ljubičić cannot be more committed to winning Wimbledon than Federer is. Federer is the player on the court, and Ljubičić is the coach is in the stands. The coach might talk to the player in the locker room, but he cannot impact the game while the game is being played.

So you cannot push, you must pull for the result, or you will fall back into the role of manager or, worse, policeman. There is nothing wrong with being a policeman or manager per se, and of course you can produce results by managing or policing people. But the pitfall is that you will have not leaders but followers or, worse, slaves around you, and your results will likely be unsustainable and will likely happen only when you are around.

Jim Collins described this in his study *Good to Great* as "a pattern we found in *every* unsustained comparison: a spectacular rise under a tyrannical disciplinarian, followed by an equally spectacular decline when the disciplinarian stepped away, leaving behind no enduring culture of discipline." A typical example was that of Rubbermaid under the helm of Stanley Gault, who was accused of being a tyrant and quipped in response, "Yes, but I'm a sincere tyrant." The result: Rubbermaid rose dramatically under Gault—it beat the market 3.6 to 1—but after he left, it lost 59 percent of its value relative to the market before being bought out by Newell.[17]

One coaching client of mine, the president of an energy company, once had to leave the office early to catch a plane to Budapest. When he arrived at the airport, he found out that the flight was cancelled, so he decided to come back to the office at 430pm—and found that most people had left for the day. It dawned upon him that the bulk of his management had stuck around in the office only when he was there—to the appearance they were working as hard as he was. They did not stay at the office based on intrinsic motivation, but because of extrinsic motivation—they felt he made them stay. That's the trap with the role of policeman.

Force is the opposite of coaching, but many of us are at the other end of force posing as coaching. I did when I was a manager (and even as a consultant working for a global consulting firm). Some boss would tell me, "Thomas, let me give you some coaching now," when I had not invited coaching at all. It was not coaching anyway; rather, it was verbal abuse posing as coaching. That is an example of force.

Power is usually defined as influence; my power is my ability to make you do something you would not do in the absence of my power. That is the usual definition of power, but that kind of power is a form of violence or, at the very least, a threat of violence, as Jonathan Sacks put it. Essentially I tell you what to do, and if you don't do it, I can impose sanctions on you, fire you, or cut some perks from you. That is a transactional way of management, coupled with force, which is not the kind of power I mean. Rabbi Sacks said it well:

> This form of violence diminishes the perpetuator and the victim alike. Because power in this sense of force is a zero-sum game. I use power to buy my freedom at the cost of yours. It is a way of getting you to do my will despite your will. It turns you into a means to my ends."[18]

In this book, power does not mean power over another person. It means the speed from idea to impact. How quickly can I move from ideation to implementation and result? That is power. Maybe we should call it impact, rather than power, because power has so many old connotations we don't want. What I mean by impact is the power to realize your commitment. You have certain commitments and your power is the speed with which you move from commitment to action and result.

Coaching vs. Management: 10 Essential Differences

Before anything else, we have to juxtapose coaching and management. If you are like me, there will be times when you will be managing your life, your enterprise, your family; then there will be times when you need to put on the coach hat. I want you to be really clear in your mind when you wear the management hat and when you wear the coaching hat. Just distinguishing these two domains clearly from one another will go a long way to you being a masterful coach.

Management and coaching are distinct paradigms, but neither is better than the other. I am not saying that management sucks and coaching is fantastic or vice versa. But there are some key differences; ten, to be precise.

#1: Management is typically knowledge-driven. Coaching is based on discovery and learning

In management, whoever knows more has more power. In a coaching context, people may or may not know. For example, I have far less expertise in the content of my clients' businesses than they do—I tell my clients openly that I will never know as much about their company or industry as they do. (I do, however, know something about human beings and what they are capable of, which led another client, an official at the U.S. State Department, to call me "a man who deserves a title that is all too often bestowed without merit, but in this case is truly deserved: miracle worker." While this is of course flattering, it is inaccurate, since my methodology is far from mysterious, as I hope to show you in this book.) In coaching, we do not have to know. In fact, the very expertise you have acquired over many years may impede your ability to get the result. When my clients are absolutely certain about something, I get suspicious. As Voltaire put it to his client, the King of Prussia, two and a half centuries ago: "Doubt is not a pleasant condition; but certainty is absurd."[19]

#2: Management is about content and information. Coaching is about context and transformation—about opening a world

Management is about the content: What is the strategy? Who is the CEO? What is the training? What is the marketing message? That is all management. Coaching is about context, which is about: Which world-view is driving everything: the person's mindset, decisions, behaviors and actions? And will that world-view lead to success, or do I need to open a new world?

You could say that management is about information; coaching is about transformation—in the sense of seeing reality in a new way. Again, at the end of any coaching conversation with my own coach, I have the sense of looking at the situation I face in a new way. The conversation does not teach me anything and yet, at the end of the conversation, I am able to see whatever challenge I bring up in a new light.

#3: Management seeks to simplify, to minimize or even avoid uncertainty. Coaching thrives on uncertainty and complexity in the pursuit of a breakthrough outcome

Related to its focus on knowing, management is concerned with bringing order to things, with maximizing predictability. We live in an unpredictable world, a so-called VUCA world of volatility, uncertainty, complexity and ambiguity. Management basically wants to forecast and increase the visibility and predictability of the future—while minimizing chaos and complexity. Coaching, by contrast, thrives on complexity. Coaching is not about having the answer, but about tackling complexity successfully and taking action. You might end up with bigger questions than those you asked in the beginning. Management is about answers; coaching is about exploration.

#4: Management is about control. Coaching is about empowerment and unleashing

Management, to minimize uncertainty, emphasizes control and order; it is based on being, or at least appearing to be, in command of the situation. The task of managers is to avoid chaos. Coaching is based on empowering and unleashing people, which may well generate creative chaos. Chaos is welcome in a coaching context. (Of course the chaos cannot be random but must be in behalf of producing a business result. One senior executive had a long-standing conflict with a direct report who felt misunderstood by him. He was in the midst of complaining once again about the subordinate when I decided to cut through the Gordian knot. I asked him spontaneously to call the direct report on the phone, and coached both of them through resolving their misunderstandings and differences. The phone call was a disruption to the lives of both executives, but by the end of the call they had built the basis for a genuine partnership.)

In the paradigm of coaching, we have no concern for

maintaining order or being in control or looking good. Our eye is solely on the ball called "produce the result." If dancing on the table or shouting the word "banana" over and over again produces the result, so be it. This is tremendously freeing, since the coach is free to be herself or himself at any given time. As a coach, you don't have to save face, you don't have to be smart, you don't have to look good. Your task is simply to enable the client to succeed, and whatever pathway leads to that outcome—as long as the pathway is legal and ethical—is permissible. (Two clients even fell in love, not with each other but each of them with another person, in two different decades. Both times were perfect for the coaching objectives—suddenly each of them became less rigid, more open to ideas and to their people, and less obsessed with controlling every detail of the operation. It was good news for everybody around them. But no guarantee that this will happen to your clients too.)

In management, you want to manage what comes across your desk, minimize the chaos, and control the situation. In coaching, you want to unleash the person; you want to have them go beyond their limits and be out of control. Well, not totally out of control. It is a little bit like being on a whitewater rafting canoe: You are constantly on the edge or beyond your comfort zone, but you are still achieving the goal of going down the river and getting to your destination.

#5: Management is about analysis. Coaching is about making sense of things

I recently received coaching by my business partner, Philippe. Yes, Philippe provided some analysis of the situation, but in essence he allowed me to make sense of things, and at the end of the conversation, I did not necessarily have a better analysis, but it started making sense, and I was able to devise my own solution.

By the way, when the player develops his or her own solution, it is much more sustainable than if the coach persuades the player of a solution, no matter how brilliant. Why? Because the player *owns* the solution. Philippe never told me what to do, what to think. He led me to think for myself.

#6: Management is concerned with changing or managing the circumstances. Coaching is concerned not with the circumstances but with the future

Management is based on responding optimally to circumstances. A causal link exists between our circumstances and what we can produce. In coaching, circumstances are taken into account, but have no causal power over outcomes. In coaching, we act inconsistent with the circumstances. Coaching is "un-reason-able": no reason is acceptable for losing. There are no excuses. New York Knicks coach Jeff Van Gundy said it this way: "You can make all the excuses for yourself and for your team, and they do absolutely no good. In the end, no one cares. Instead of making excuses for why they can't, give them reasons why they can."[20]

As coach, you are the advocate of the player's future. You never stop being committed to his or her commitments. You are standing for the future when the player wants to give up. You remind the player of the future they committed to, even—and especially—when they forget, and we all tend to forget our future in the heat of the action. That is what Philippe did. He basically gave me the perspective from the future. What are the long-term consequences of your decision? What are the implications one year from now, five years from now? What are your life commitments, and hence the implications for your entire life? That is what coaching is concerned with, not merely with your problems right now and how you can fix them. Coaching assists with problem solving, too—but not by reacting to the problem and fixing it. Coaching aims to look at the problem proactively, by looking at the problem from the future, which often affords a solution-oriented vantage point.

#7: Management is based on predicting and forecasting. Coaching is based not on prediction but on promise

Managers try to get a handle on what will happen in the future as precisely and accurately as possible. Promises, by contrast, are by definition unpredictable. When you promise, if the promise deserves the name, you may or may not have a pathway to the fulfillment of your promise. Gary Hamel and C.K. Prahalad's seminal article "Strategic Intent"[21] specifically stipulates that players formulate and declare an ambition that produces a "strategic misfit," a gap between the current reality and the desired future. A strategic intent that deserves the name should completely outstrip the player's current competence. For example, when Sir Colin Marshall declared that British Airways would become the premier airline, the airline's acronym "BA" stood in the public's mind for... "Bloody Awful." That's what I call a bold strategic intent.

#8: Management is about rules and compliance. Coaching is about values

There is nothing wrong with rules. I am saying this as a Swiss person: I like rules. In Switzerland, we have perfected the rules since 1291, the year we founded the country. We have been around for over 730 years, all those rules make sense and virtually everybody complies with the rules, and when everybody complies, you have a very efficient machine. But that is management, not coaching. Coaching is about your core values—what you believe in, what is important to you, what matters to you.

#9: Management looks at human resources or human capital. Coaching looks at the whole human being

As a coach, I am coaching a human being. In order to keep Roger Federer on a winning path, his coach Ivan Ljubičić does not care only about the technique, hitting the ball right or even only about the results in Wimbledon. Federer's technique is pretty much flawless anyway. Rather, Ljubičić has to keep in mind all of Federer's life, his financial life, his four children, his marriage —basically whatever is going on in the context of his performance. His concern cannot be about the behaviors or the results in a vacuum.

#10: Finally, management is (and should be) concerned with results. Coaching is concerned with success, which includes the results, but it is broader than the results
You could say that success equals results with accomplishment and satisfaction. The coach needs to be at least as committed to the player's winning as the player is. This includes that the coach must tell the player if the player's promise is full of baloney. But rather than saying, "This is a terrible idea," the coach would say: "I don't quite get that this promise is grounded. Tell me more about how you intend to fulfill it." So even when the coach sees that a promise cannot be pulled off, s/he intends to empower the speaker of the promise to come up with feasibility. (One Australian client wanted to go public within six months, and I had to challenge them over and over until they saw that this was not a promise but a dream at this particular stage of the company.)

If the above sounds a bit abstract, no worries—I will give you a step-by-step process for how to implement these principles below.

Though coaching and management are two distinct paradigms, they are not entirely separate—often coaches must manage and managers must coach—and again, neither domain is better than the other, which would be like saying that air is better than water or vice versa. The management hat and the coaching hat are both required if you want to lead effectively, and you better know at any given time which hat you are wearing. Remember, breathing under water is bad for you.

This distinction between management and coaching is crucial for two reasons. First, whenever there is stress in the organization, or whenever we are stressed, we might be tempted to revert to familiar but outdated behaviors, behaviors that worked in the past when there was cheese down that tunnel. For example, we go back to command and control, or to what's predictable, or to just managing results.

Management vs. Coaching: 10 Essential Differences

Management Hat	Coach Hat
Knowing	Learning, discovery
Information, content	Transformation, context
Simplifying, minimizing uncertainty, maximizing predictability	Mastering complexity, welcoming uncertainty in service of a breakthrough outcome
Controlling	Empowering, unleashing
Analyzing	Sense-making
Circumstances, track record determines the future	Future determines the actions now
Prediction, forecast	Promise, vision, strategic intent
Rules and compliance	Values
Human resources, human capital	The whole human being
Results	Success
Manager is boss	Player is boss, coach is sparring partner

Table 1. Coaching vs. Management: 10 Essential Differences. Neither domain is better than the other; but you need to be cognizant of which domain you're in. Water and air are both good things, but breathing under water is usually harmful.

Second, "the heartland of the problem and the essential dilemma," said my colleague Mick Crews, a former top executive at the shipping company Cunard Ellerman who became a consultant, is that "it is difficult for business to operate according to a coaching paradigm when the whole of business is not based on coaching but on the maximization of assets."[22]

Mick made an important point. We should all be vigilant of falling into the trap of maximizing growth at the expense of people power. Asset growth and coaching might clash with one another. Call me an incorrigible optimist, but I don't see a contradiction between coaching and results anymore. Effective coaching, done in the way I present in this book, marries a concern for people (including their satisfaction, well-being and fulfillment) with a concern for breakthrough performance.

In fact, when you work with people such that they go beyond themselves, they are one and the same. The next chapter will show you how to build high-performance relationships that integrate the two. But again, in order to distinguish the Coaching relationship, we need to first say what it is *not*.

To all those who are raring to go and feel we are going backwards here, I want you to remember the Michelangelo. In order to create his sculpture of David out of a slab of stone, the Renaissance artist had to take away everything that was not David. So the act of creation consists of distinguishing what you want from everything else. We will do the same with the Coaching relationship in the next chapter.

CHAPTER 3. SPARRING PARTNER: WHAT'S THE DIFFERENCE?

Don't walk in front of me
I may not follow
Don't walk behind me
I may not lead
Walk beside me
And just be my friend
—Albert Camus

Mick Crews, the top-manager-turned-coach, made another important distinction: between team coaches, for example in soccer (football outside the United States) and individual coaches, say for a tennis player or a boxer. "Manchester United's coach brings out the best in players but trades players quickly once they're off the boil," Mick said. "In tennis it is more genuine: Players hire coaches. The player is the boss. In team games it doesn't work like this."[23] In team games, just like in companies, the roles of coach and of boss are conflated—a dangerous mix. This brings us to the first differentiator of the coaching relationship.

The Coach Is Not the Boss
In most companies, management asks that people "buy into" its decisions, policies and strategies. In management, decisions have usually been taken already, and people are expected to accept them and comply with them. Because of this practice, we now have buzzwords like "cascading through the organization."

You have a hierarchical structure, and the behaviors of the participants reflect the hierarchy. The manager is the boss, which requires a lower level of responsibility from the subordinate and often leads to management by excuses ("Well, I couldn't do it because ... happened" or "It's not my fault that ... happened.")

In the domain of coaching, people are not buying anything. People are the owners—or not, in which case we will not take a proposed action. There is ownership or nothing. In coaching, both player and coach are willing to be totally responsible for producing the outcome. And ultimately, the player—just like Roger Federer—is the author.

In my coaching, this is my highest priority—ensuring that the client has ownership of the entire coaching process. I have a fine-tuned radar for clients "just checking it out" or "going along for the ride" or being there "because my boss 're-commended' it." I would rather refuse the coaching process—and forego the hefty fees that come with it—than accept a player caught in the role of what I call a tourist, or worse, a victim or hostage. When I sense that the client is not driving the process, I stop and reestablish the ownership by asking what the players wants and what we're doing it for in the first place. (I also ask if the player has any doubts or reservations about the coaching. I found that if the player can express all that might stand in the way of their full ownership, their commitment is more genuine.)

The cool thing about coaching is that you cannot force it on anyone. Coaching is optional. It happens by choice. So if your boss or a colleague says to you (as they did to me when I was a young manager), "Listen up, I'm gonna give you some coaching now," it sounds like the word "coaching" in that sentence could be easily replaced by "whipping."

At a top-tier multinational energy company, the headquarters in Houston asked me to coach the top manager of their European subsidiary. They simply planned to impose coaching on someone they saw as a difficult top manager. I made it clear to them that coaching is not merely a nicer word for forcing or dominating or managing. When I called the European top manager in Hamburg—actually I reached him on his carphone, he was sitting in the Mercedes on the German autobahn en route to Munich, at a speed of some 300 kilometers per hour, fortunately he had a chauffeur—he told me: "I don't like touchy-feely, touching hands, Billy Graham revival, public vomiting of feelings." Whatever he meant by that, the burden was on me to clarify what coaching was and what it wasn't. I made it clear that I was not out to change him (you can't change another person anyway unless they want to change), that he was brilliant the way he was, that if he never changed it would be fine by me, that all we could do together was perhaps to open some new dimensions he might not have previously considered.

The point is, the client is the boss. And by "client" I do not mean the company, even if the company foots the bills. I mean the individual client. Coaching cannot be hierarchical. Player and coach are a full partners.

The Coach Is Not the Friend
As a friend, I might console you. I might be there for you, listen to your problems, and commiserate. There is a distinction between friend and coach because a friend tends to go into agreement with the friend and commiserate, "Oh yeah, that really sucks, I understand." The coach might empathize, but is not merely a friend. The coach is not paid for agreeing with the player, lest he or she will lose the kind of toughness a coach needs to jettison the niceties for the sake of the player's commitments and future.

Although the coach loves the player, the coach is not a buddy, a friend, or a supporter. (I know of CEOs who use their peers as sounding boards, and that can be very helpful, especially when peers confront similar issues. But the peer then takes on the role of confidant and/or mentor who can share his or her experience with you. While coaching may incorporate this aspect, it is not the same as the coach-player relationship.)

Dr. Thomas D. Zweifel

The Coach Is Not the Shrink

Sometimes people who meet me and who don't know my work say, "Ah, you're a business shrink." I take that as a big compliment; but it's inaccurate. I never had a formal psychology education. I understand a lot about psychology, though, partly because the field interests me tremendously and partly because I have experimented on myself by undergoing psychoanalysis ever since 2007. I also understand a lot about behavioral psychology, behavioral economics. But I am clearly not a shrink. The main distinction is this: A shrink would help you understand why you are the way you are. The shrink would give you access to the deep root causes that cause you to behave or feel a certain way today, and that could be useful, by the way. Just like a friend, a shrink can be useful, even life-changing.

Yes, psychology and coaching overlap. Just like a psychologist, the coach delves often into the most intimate regions of the player's emotional and mental life to explore hidden motives or fears or other root causes of behavioral patterns. Over the years, my own psychoanalyst has given me access to my own deep-seated, invisible, subterranean patterns I was blind to. Such an exploration can be extremely helpful in becoming a self-determined human being. So I have nothing against shrinks, on the contrary; a skillful shrink can add tremendous value to your quality of life. But there are two important differences. First, a shrink—except for some strands of psychology, namely so-called positive psychology—would usually be more concerned with unearthing the past that caused the present than with the future that can cause the present. Most psychologists are not concerned with the future. The bottom line is, at least in my coaching framework, a shrink is not a coach.

Second, my psychoanalyst to this day calls me his "patient"—even though I have zero pathology, as he himself has attested for years. The word "patient" comes from the Latin *patiens*, "the sufferer," so it connotes that the person is in need of a remedy. All too often the term "coaching" is used as a euphemism to mask the true intention of management: to correct a failing executive. But true coaching—at least the kind that I believe in—is not remedial. A coach is not a doctor or therapist trying to "fix" a patient. One client initially held coaching in a remedial framework (not least because his superiors had made it clear that "this is his last chance—he will either improve out of this coaching or his days are numbered"), so I first had to dissuade him from that notion. "What's wrong with me?" he said. "Everybody says I need coaching. Why do I need coaching? Who is as productive as me? But it's not good if I boast." I explained that my coaching approach has nothing to do with fixing people. My client was already great—in fact, this particular client was a champion, a racehorse, a winner. My job was not to fix him, but to reveal a new possibility in his work/life, a possible future that may have been buried under his decade-old routines.

The Coach Is Not the Expert
Experts usually know more than the person to whom they provide their expertise. A coach does not need to know more. In fact, if he or she knows more, then it usually gets in the way because then they think, "I know what is good for you," but the coach does not and cannot know what is good for the other person. If the coach has any expertise, they should put that expertise away, lock it up, and encounter the player newly, without knowing anything, with a beginner's mind. Those moments when I think I know something, I would basically ask the player, "Do you want my advice now?" And if the player says yes, I will say, "I am taking off my coach hat now and putting on my advisor hat, to give you some advice based on my experience, but please do not mistake this for coaching because, as a coach, I know nothing, and I am not paid for knowing. I am not paid for my expertise. I am paid for not knowing what will work for you. You are the only person who will know what solution works for you."

    Years ago, my colleague Allan Cohen drew a distinction that was very useful for my work. He said there are basically three types of consulting: Content Consulting where the consultant brings content to the client, for example a marketing message or an IT service; Process Consulting where the consultant is paid for the design or management of a process, for example a reengineering process or a system integration; and finally, Contextual Consulting where the consultant reveals a hidden, past-based driver or culture in the client organization and, if needed, helps the client design a new driver from the future. The contextual consultant, or the coach, does not need domain expertise to do their job. In fact domain expertise could be an impediment since the job is to disrupt a mindset—and it's easier to disrupt a mindset if you come from outside the system.

In fact the coach need not even be a great player. Look once again at Ivan Ljubicic, who started as Roger Federer's coach in 2016. While Ljubicic is certainly a good tennis player himself, he could never be a match for Federer. Ljubicic's expertise lay not in playing better than Federer, but rather in the quality of his observations and his conversations with the player. An even more extreme example is the famous Olympic gymnastics coach Bela Karolyi, who "couldn't do a split if his life depended on it."[24] The same was true for my coaching: When I met the president of the first-tier energy company above, I told him frankly that I would never understand his business as well as he did—not even close. When I started coaching him, I was 40 years old while he was 60. He had spent over thirty years building his know-how. I could never match that.

"I know nothing," I told him (perhaps a bit of an understatement to get my point across). "I will never be as experienced as you are in the domain of your business because you've been around for over thirty years." The president was 62 years old, and I was 40. "I would never have the temerity to advise you on your business. You know much more about that than I would ever know." Instead, I told him, "I understand something about leadership and performance. I know something about human beings. I know something about conversations, and I could probably ask some questions that would open some new possibilities or new ways of looking at things." My added value could be as a sparring partner, a confidant, a consigliere if you will, who could help him reveal blind spots and open up some new dimensions that he might have never have considered before.

That sold him on the coaching. It was not my trying to impress him with everything I knew. It made it safe for him because I was not competing with him. It was disarming that I was humble (with the right dose of self-confidence), and that helped him trust me as a coach, and it made it okay that I was a lot younger than him. I also took the wind out of his sails, since he was probably asking himself, "What does a young guy like that want to tell me about life?"

At the end of the conversation he did sign on, which led to a fruitful working relationship that lasted for many years. I ended up coaching him not only on company strategy and his leadership and performance as president, but also on his personal life. He said he felt comfortable telling me things he didn't even tell his wife. After a difficult divorce, he even invited me to his wedding, which for somebody like him, an old-style authoritarian leader, was a real breakthrough. Much of his openness came from the fact that at the beginning, I had distinguished being an expert from being a coach.

At the end of the Coaching-In-Action process, he gave me one of the highest compliments I ever received: "I wish I had had your tools 35 years ago, when I was starting out."

The Coach Is Not the Teacher or Trainer
Much like experts, teachers and trainers know more (usually, and hopefully) than their students or trainees. They are hired to impact certain skills or impart certain knowledge to their students or trainees. That is not the case in coaching. Coaching is not training, nor is it education, even though sometimes there might be some training or education as a side effect. The player might learn something about politics, for example, or about communication, or about psychology, but in that moment, that

is not coaching, it is teaching or training. I want you to be vigilant not to fall into this trap of, "I know something. Here is my experience, and I am going to show you how it works." That is a big pitfall, and it is usually less useful for the player. Just be vigilant not to fall into that trap. Of course nothing prevents you from coaching somebody even if you do know more about a certain field. Just avoid coaching from that knowledge because knowing is not coaching.

A second difference: Trainers and teachers have power over their trainees or students. Trainers can impose their methods on the trainees; teachers can punish students with bad grades. The coach, by contrast, can only make suggestions and ultimately defers to the client. The player is and remains the boss. It was Becker, not Tiriac, who was ultimately accountable for winning Wimbledon, and he could fire Tiriac at any time—and eventually did. (As you can tell by now, I am a sort of tennis aficionado.)

In the coaching relationship, the player is the one who will make the decisions; the player is the one who can even cancel the coaching relationship at any time if it doesn't empower them. They are the client, the judge, so they are right. If they don't like it, the coach cannot say, "Well, I'm such a great coach, you should definitely keep me on. I am telling you how it is." The coach is beside, not above the player.

The Coach Is Not the Mentor

Mentoring is so close to coaching that the two activities often get confused with each other, but a mentor is generally older and more experienced than the mentee. The mentor knows more, the mentee less. The mentor says in essence, "I've been around for ten or thirty years. I know something about this. Here is my experience. Here are the best practices that I've picked up in my decades of leadership or management." It can be very useful to have a mentor like this, but that is not coaching in the strict sense.

Mentors usually can do things better than mentees. The

Olympic gymnastics coach Bela Karolyi, by contrast, could not do a split if his life depended on it. Or consider Maxwell Perkins, the great Scribner's editor, who found, nurtured, and published such writers as F. Scott Fitzgerald, Ernest Hemingway, and Thomas Wolfe. "Perkins has the intangible faculty of giving you confidence in yourself and the book you are writing," one of his writers said in a 1944 *New Yorker* Profile. "He never tells you what to do," another writer said. "Instead, he suggests to you, in an extraordinarily inarticulate fashion, what you want to do yourself."[25]

To my colleague Lelia O'Connor, mentoring is a modeling behavior: "Do what I do to be successful." Coaching, on the other hand, is a generative, productive relationship characterized by co-creation.[26] I have had the privilege of coaching corporate leaders who were many years older than me. They had more experience than me in life as well as in their business discipline. But they invariably told me that the coaching made a big difference in their work and their lives. One of them called me "an extraordinary thinking partner in preparing and debriefing activities and getting the highest leverage out of them. You don't believe what you can achieve."

The Coach Is Not the Advisor

Please give me some good advice in your next letter.
I promise not to follow it.
—Edna St. Vincent Millay

I cannot overstate the importance of this principle. You want to check yourself at all times: Are you urging to give advice? I would say this especially to the men out there. Permit me to generalize for a moment. Men, according to John Gray, author of *Men are from Mars, Women are from Venus,* usually hear about a problem and immediately want to solve it. They see the answer. They jump to, "We just need to do XYZ." When men are working together, that works well: We just fix the problem and move on. On the other hand, when women tell you a problem, they seldom want an immediate fix; they mostly want to be heard, understood, empathized with. When my wife tells me an issue she is facing, I easily forget all I know about coaching and slip into fix-it mode: "Just try X" or "Have you tried Y?" In coaching, what I call the advice machine is counter-productive.

Coaching means essentially to step back from that urge to fix things and instead to conduct an inquiry. Resist the urge to give advice, to give the solution. My friend and colleague Peter Block, author of the seminal book *Flawless Consulting*, made the same point succinctly: "Resist helping people."[27]

People, especially those in the service industries, might gasp at Peter's suggestion; he might even be accused of callousness. But his point is pivotal. Your job is not merely to help but to empower; to facilitate an inquiry at the end of which the player will have his or her own solution. Such a solution is infinitely better than the one you had in mind. Why? Because it is *their* solution; they created it, they came up with it. It is usually much more actionable, more empowering, more sustainable and more likely to be implemented than if it were imposed on them, even though everybody knows that all your solutions are always brilliant. (Okay, that was Swiss irony.)

The coach is not an advisor. Advice is not the same as coaching, although the coach may occasionally give advice to the client. But it's not the answers you give your client—it's the right questions that will open up new vistas, a new world, for him or her.

Yes, coaching *can* include elements of all these relationships: mentor, psychologist/therapist, best friend, advisor, trainer, teacher, or expert. But coaching is a distinction. And as a coach, you better be aware which hat you're wearing at any given time.

Bottom line: The coach is not the boss, the friend, the shrink, the expert, the teacher/trainer, the mentor or the advisor. Now that we got clear what coaching is *not*, we can finally turn to what coaching *is*.

CHAPTER 4. DISTINCTION: WHAT COACHING IS

We have to believe in free will: we have no choice.
—Isaac Bashevis Singer

In the last chapter, you saw what coaching is not. And at the outset of the book, I promised you that coaching is the solution for finding freedom, power (as in impact) and peace of mind. So, what *is* coaching?

Webster's New Universal Unabridged Dictionary defines a "coach" as a person who trains an athlete or a team of athletes; a playing or non-playing member of the team who signals instructions to base runners and batters (the baseball usage); a private tutor who prepares a student for an examination; and a person who instructs an actor or singer. "To coach" means to give instruction or advice, in the capacity of a coach; to act as a coach; to study with or be instructed by a coach. These definitions tell us about the outcomes that coaching produces; but since they do not give access to what coaching is or how it occurs, they are not really useful for our purposes.

Let us instead return to the original meaning of the word "coach." A coach, as the term was originally used, is a vessel that enables people to get from point A to point B. That definition comes much closer to who we are when we coach someone. Like a vessel, we need to be underneath those whom we coach. We enable them to get somewhere that they might not reach on their own. They may even take us for granted sometimes. A coach only shows up when coaching breaks down. When things go smoothly, coaches tend to be invisible.

I want you to conduct a small self-reflection to unearth one or several coaches in your life (whether or not you saw them as a coach then). Can you think of one of the things you have accomplished in your life, something outstanding? It could have been in your professional life that you did something beyond the norm. It could be in sports, it could be in school, it could be in your family.

My next question is, Who was coaching you? I am using the word 'coaching' although you might not be aware that it was coaching at the time. Who was around you? Who was in the background that allowed you to achieve the success? If I look at my life and the successes, the productivity and breakthroughs I have had, my breakthroughs in sports—running a sub-3-hour marathon for example—or commercial breakthroughs in any field of my life, it was always thanks to somebody who was coaching me, and I would like you to look at that person in your life. What was present?

Lab: When Did You Have a Great Coach?

Recall a time in your life when you accomplished something great. This moment of peak performance could be in sports, in school, in your professional life, or elsewhere. What was (were) the accomplishment(s)?

Who was there for you as a coach?

What worked about your interactions with that coach (key success factors)?

Whatever and whomever you wrote down in this self-reflection (and even if you wrote down nothing), your coach was likely an intimate confidant who made it safe for you to be yourself; someone who was committed to your success; someone who held the line on your commitment even when you wanted to give up.

Probably what was present was an unwavering, unyielding commitment to who you are, to your commitments and to your future. Your coach likely had an unconditional commitment to the client's success—he or she had to believe the player could win. To take an example from the distant past, when Andy Roddick hired Brad Gilbert as his coach back in 2003, Gilbert agreed immediately, saying it had to be "somebody I felt like had a chance to be No. 1 in the world."[28] (When he said it, Gilbert meant it. But a conviction is of course no guarantee for success.)

Probably you felt safe, free of judgment, free of evaluation. In the conversation, there was nothing taboo; there was nothing irrelevant. Whatever you said mattered to the other person.

Who has ever had another person one hundred percent committed to his/her success; somebody who will never let them down, somebody whom they can tell their most secret thoughts?

Take senior or top managers. The higher you rise in the hierarchy, the fewer people you can trust, and the more you have to second-guess. "CEOs don't really have anyone they can talk to," explains Atlanta pastor and author Ike Reighard, who became a touchstone for numerous entrepreneurs. "Sometimes they're the most well-connected people and yet the loneliest you will ever meet. It's hard to have trusting relationships when people so often want something from you."[29]

One of my clients, the CEO of a family company founded by two people after World War II that today boasts a workforce of 12,000, met with me secretly on a monthly basis over three years. He never quite knew who would use whatever he said against him. With whom could he share half-baked or even crazy ideas without being laughed at? Whom could he tell that he didn't know something without being seen as incompetent? Whom could he tell anything without a nagging afterthought that the person might somehow use that statement against him? He selected me as his sparring partner—someone outside the system, who had no hidden agenda, someone who would never use what he said against him, someone who was 100 percent committed to his success.

Types of Coaching

The role of coach is unusual for most leaders or managers. After all, our responsibility is to manage, to produce results, not to dabble in people's internal process. But a thorough understanding of coaching can cause a quantum leap in our effectiveness in empowering others.

Marshall Goldsmith and Howard Morgan distinguished three types of coaching: behavioral change coaching, personal productivity coaching, and "energy" coaching.[30] Later, they offered five distinctions of leadership coaching: strategic, organizational change/execution, leadership development, personal/life planning, and behavioral.[31] These distinctions are useful for narrowing down what the client wants to focus on. In my experience that focus can easily shift in the course of a coaching relationship, and often two or more types of coaching overlap. The player might start in one place, for example strategic or change management or performance, only to discover an intense life issue that stands in the way of success and requires a behavioral or mindset shift. The CEO above, for example, faced the need to convince his Executive Committee of a system-wide strategy innovation, only to find out that he needed to look at the challenge in a new way and that his desire for harmony got in the way of making tough decisions.

Or the other way around: The player starts with a behavioral issue and discovers that the root cause is strategic. One client, a banking executive, set out to work with me on his public speaking, his ability to present information and to persuade audiences—but in the course of the coaching we discovered that the organization suffered from serious strategic misalignment, which meant he had no chance, no matter how good his persuasion skills, unless he addressed the underlying strategic fragmentation.

To me, Goldsmith's and Morgan's types of coaching are more like a repertoire, a menu of options that coach and player can choose from. They should choose at any moment whichever type of coaching yields the highest leverage.

Being a Coach

Number one, before you think about what to do, you have to think about who you are. Being a coach is basically in your mind. My marathon trainer, when I still ran marathons, used to tell me that only 10 percent of running the marathon is in the legs and arms, your technique, how you are moving. The other 90 percent happens in your head. These 90 percent is your attitude. What is your mindset as you are running? Are you seeing the marathon as something to survive, to get through? Or are you in the zone, taking it step by step, living it up each moment? That determines your performance.

Safety Net

A coach has an unconditional commitment to the client's success (again, not merely the results but the overall success, which includes the results but is broader than the results). The coach is the sparring partner. You are somebody the player can say anything to and it's safe. It's confidential. You will never use whatever he or she says or does against him or her. You will never disclose anything.

I made a mistake only once in my career when I disclosed something the CEO above told me in confidence: Because I assumed it was public knowledge, I told the HR chief. It took me several months to restore trust with the CEO. And I had learned my lesson—I never did something like that again.

There is nothing stupid; no question, no concern, no statement is stupid or evaluated. You are not judging anything the player says. Around you, he or she has total freedom to be. And that is highly valuable.

Committed Listening
The coach is committed to the fulfillment of any promise the player declares, no matter what it is. (Well, within legal and ethical bounds—if the player declares he wants to rob a bank, build a prostitution ring or do anything similarly unsavory, the coach should refuse to participate and withdraw from the relationship.)

Even better: Whatever the player says, the coach can interpret as a commitment. This takes the player's word seriously and puts the player on notice that his or her word is not just idle chatter but counts. If the player says, "I must go to work," then the coach can say, "Interesting, did you notice you used the word *must*? Are you committed to that? Are you committed to being a slave who must go to work? Is that your choice?" Or if a CEO complains about his Executive Committee being "a bunch of incompetents," the question, "Are you committed to that?" will stop the recreational complaining in its tracks and instead open a conversation about possible interventions. "Language is the house of being," Martin Heidegger said, so the language we use creates reality. Whatever comes out of the player's mouth can be heard as a commitment and the coach listens as a committed listener.

> **Tip.** Listen for the gold. Our brains are conditioned—for about the last 10,000 years, more or less, ever since we walked out of our cave, a stranger stood outside, and we had to decide within a split second whether that stranger was friend or foe—to listen for what's wrong, what's missing, what could be dangerous. Thousands of years ago such a reflex would be appropriate; today, unless you find yourself in a lawless place or the

> jungle, it's not. So be sure to listen not for the dirt but for the gold.

Straight Talk
The coach talks straight. You will not mince words. You are not nice to the player. You are not diplomatic. The coach is whomever he or she needs to be to empower the player to perform at their best. Not abusive, obviously, but the coach does his or her best to rip apart existing patterns of behavior or mindsets, and to question outdated mindsets not consistent with where the player wants to go. Since 90 percent of running the marathon is really in the runner's head, the coach might have to do some "mind surgery" (as my friend Michael Jascz used to put it) as well.

As a coach, you are focused on telling the unvarnished truth, rather than on what is popular or permissible—or what will ensure you keep the contract with the player. This is a tough one. You have to watch out for the pitfall of selling out on the truth to keep your mandate. Remember that the player —especially if he or she is a top or senior manager—is likely not used to hearing the truth. Not unlike the French Sun King Louis XIV, top managers are often surrounded by yes-men (or yes-women). who hesitate to tell them inconvenient truths—for fear of losing their job or losing access to power. You are quite possibly the only person who gives them the facts straight.

Bottom Line: When You Wear Your Coach Hat
To sum up what it means to serve as a coach:

You are the player's ***full partner***. (The term "partner" comes closest to what a coach is, since coach and player co-create the future together.)

You exhibit ***ruthless compassion***. Compassion: You empathize with what it takes the player to be a player, to be in the hot seat, to live as a leader day after day. Ruthless: Like a doctor, you will not hesitate to administer tough medicine if necessary, and you will call the player on any games he or she might play to avoid being who they need to be to succeed. You know that only this combination of "tough love" produces the mix from which comes extraordinary performance. As a coach, you constantly challenge and go beyond what exists already.

You provide *new ways of seeing*. As executive coach Stanley Goss put it, "there are two people working on your success—two sets of eyes helping you see what you don't see."[32] Rather than getting stuck in talking about the circumstances, a coach provides new ways of looking at those circumstances that have the world show up in a new way for the player.

You distinguish yourself by *authentic, honest and full communication*. There is nothing that the player could not confide in you. And there is nothing that you have to withhold because the player might pay the bills, or because the player might hold some power over you, or because you might fear the loss of the relationship (meaning the contract).

You *generate demand for your coaching*. In other words, you never provide coaching unless there is a request for coaching—never, not once. And you cannot take demand for coaching for granted. If you built it yesterday or an hour ago, it might have vanished into thin air since then. For every new intervention, you have to first check whether demand for coaching is still strong, and if not, rebuild it.

The Ten Commandments for Competent Coaching
As a coach, test-drive these guidelines for success and, if they make sense, see if you can adopt them permanently:

1. You are committed to the fulfillment of any promise you listen to.
2. You need not accept a promise. You may decline a promise that seems not grounded or seems to point in the wrong direction.
3. You listen for agreements or actions going out of existence. You keep a record of all promises made, and you follow up on each.
4. You don't listen to a promise that is not written

down by the player making the promise.
5. You catch lies, slippery revocations of promises ("I didn't really mean it...") or non-measurable results.
6. You are on a constant quest to determine what is missing for the fulfillment of the player's promise.
7. You look for opportunities to provide coaching to speed up the fulfillment of the promise. You look to add velocity and urgency.
8. You meet regularly, on agreed-upon intervals, with the player to debrief the past period (usually the last month or week) and set up the next.
9. The debriefs include what the player accomplished and what was not accomplished, what worked and what did not work, and what is missing for meeting the player's objectives that can be put in place.
10. The bottom line about great coaches is: It's not what you *know* (in fact what you know can get in the way of coaching). It's who you *are* and what you *do* that matters.

Lab: When Were You a Great Coach for Someone?

> Recall a moment in your life when you helped someone else accomplish something great. This moment of peak performance could be in sports, in school, in your professional life, or elsewhere. What was the accomplishment?
>
>
> What worked about your interactions with that player (what were the key success factors)?

As we come to the end of this chapter, I want to point

out a possible pitfall around selecting coaches: collusion. Since people are only human, they are prone to minimize the confrontation with their promises. They might select the person who is "the nicest," with whom they have "such good chemistry"—but who will also most easily let them off the hook, rather than the one who will say and do whatever it takes to ensure their success. One way of avoiding this pitfall is to reward coaches for the performance of their players (or to punish them for the lack thereof). But that would immediately bring up other problems—for example that the coach might be more committed to the player's objective than the player, which is a no-go since it violates the ground rules above. The only solution I see for this pitfall is the coach's vigilance: Ask yourself at all times, Am I taking the path of least resistance and withholding truth I should speak to power? Or am I giving the hard love the player needs to go beyond themselves? It's a question you can never quite tick off your checklist.

CHAPTER 5. CAT-AND-MOUSE: CATCHING COACHING OPPORTUNITIES

*Eighty percent of success
is showing up.*
—Woody Allen

Now that we know what coaching is that deserves the name, we can actually see how you start coaching somebody. You cannot simply open your mouth and start coaching. It is pivotal that you first reveal an opening for coaching. You have to create a demand and in this chapter, I want to show you how. Basically, that is why I call it cat and mouse, how can you sit like a cat in front of the mouse hole and actually see whether the cat is coming out so that you can catch the mouse. I am not sure this is the best possible metaphor but that is what I came up with.

Remember, you cannot coach someone without their demand for coaching. Without demand, your coaching, in the eyes of the recipient, is mere noise—a disturbance in his or her life. If you coach somebody without their demand, they don't understand. "What the heck are doing? Why are you talking to me like this? I didn't ask you to."

You cannot push coaching on somebody. Coaching without demand is usually counterproductive, it can even be destructive, and it will not produce any result other than people being irritated and annoyed with you. They have to invite you in. And in order to build demand for coaching, you first need to see and reveal opportunities for coaching.

What Is an Opening for Coaching?
Let's look at what constitutes an opening or an opportunity for coaching. If a customer complains, that could be an opening for coaching because something happened and it was not so great, so we could talk about this and perhaps we could debrief the incident and find different ways of looking at this.

I am actually not going to go yet into how you present the opening for coaching to the player. For now, it's just about how you see the opening for coaching. How do you reveal it, discover it? It could be some form of a crisis that the person is facing where they don't know what to do and whatever their existing tool or their existing approach is not quite cutting the mustard. But also a problem, a breakdown or a crisis could offer an opening for coaching.

But the occasion doesn't have to be negative, it can also be positive. If I have just achieved a big success—perhaps I have just met a business objective or been promoted to a new role—and I suddenly feel like there is so much more available, then that could be an opening for coaching. To use my favorite friend Roger Federer again: If Roger wins Wimbledon, then the coaching opening could be how he could win all four grand slams in a given year. How could he win the French open, which is on sand? How could he win the US open, which is on a hard court? So an achievement can provide an opening for coaching. Similarly, a promotion can be an opening for coaching. Suddenly the person has been promoted and they are now at a much higher level of leadership. In some way, they have other people to lead and that new role can be another opening for coaching.

More traditionally, an annual performance review could be an opening for coaching. Instead of going into a pure evaluation, an assessment of the person or their performance, you could actually seize that as an opening for coaching. Let's say we are an insurance company and we would like to enter China or another new market. That might be an opening for coaching.

Basically, what I want to drive home here is that almost anything could be an opening for coaching. The one exception is if it is a crisis that is so urgent that there is literally no space to think. Let's say the house is on fire or the Titanic is going under water, there is no need to say, "Hey, I can offer you some coaching" because the person is just fighting for survival and they are going under water. Such situations offer no opening for coaching because people simply have to put the fire out or make sure the boat doesn't sink and there is no space to reflect on anything.

Pretty much anything else presents an opening, including when somebody did not keep their word. Perhaps they promised something and didn't deliver or somebody else promised them something and didn't perform. That can be an opening for coaching. I coached two senior partners at a law-firm and each of them had committed to certain actions from one coaching session to the next. As is my custom in every coaching session, I followed up at the start of the following session (right after asking them what was on their mind)—and it turned out that neither had done what they had promised. This was a big opening for coaching. I asked them if this was an exception or a frequent occurrence. They said it was, to their chagrin, the rule. I asked what was missing for them to honor their word. We discovered that they suffered from a tendency to manage what's top of mind rather than managing their commitments. In fact we discovered all kinds of things, including their inability to say "no" or stick to their priorities, the firm's culture of no follow-up ("Details are boring, we are the cowboys, we want to be free to change the world"), and other raw material for coaching them and, more importantly, setting the firm on course for the future. The point is, this all came from my refusal to let them off the hook on their promises.

These openings are far from exhaustive. For example it could be a performance review (as long as the reviewer can avoid the pitfall of evaluating the person—all too often performance reviews degenerate into vehicles of domination and control). It could be a new role, a new opportunity. A great success achieved or a milestone met.

If you observe simple unease in the other person, that can be an opening for coaching too. So can chronic resistance to an invitation or to a request. (The very resistance that many leaders loathe—because they see resistance as a threat to their authority—is possible raw material for coaching.) So can a trace of suffering. Indeed, at one of my recent coaching workshops, participants identified almost any human emotion as an occasion for coaching: an angry outburst, but also withheld anger; uncertainty or insecurity; a clear position or opinion; envy or ambition; and so forth.

Listening for What Is Un-Said
Your job is to be like a flower waiting for the bee to visit your blossom. Or, if you prefer a more active image, you sit like a cat in front of the mouse hole, ready to pounce as soon as the mouse appears. Here your communication and listening skills are paramount. Human beings have two ears and one mouth, not the other way around. You were equipped with two ears and that is not accidental. Our ears are extremely important. Again, in this phase of revealing an opening for coaching, you listen vigilantly. You have a mission to discover these openings for coaching, they don't just simply appear to you—and if they do, that is an added, unexpected bonus. You have to reveal them. Your job is to recognize the opening for coaching when it appears. Otherwise you have no opportunity to go to work with the client. You need to find the gate to the village and cannot simply bomb your way in. We saw this above: You cannot use force, you cannot push yourself on the other person, you have to find the opening. That is why listening is very important.

You need to listen carefully, really hear what the person is saying, without making substantial comments at first. Whenever I start coaching, I ask the client simply: "What's on your mind?" It sounds like an innocent question, but many executives are rarely given the opportunity to express openly whatever is there for them, without anyone raising their eyebrows at them, without them being assessed or evaluated or censored in any way. "What's on your mind?" opens up this freedom of expression. You could phrase it differently and say, "What keeps you up at night?" or "What do you want to talk about right now?" or even "How are you?" (as long as you avoid falling into the trap of small talk). However you ask it, the question "What's on your mind?" is quite magical. Be sure to shut your mouth and refrain from intervening, from judging and from trying to give a solution. If you let the person talk for a while, you will reveal raw material for coaching. Then, after a few minutes, you can ask the second innocent but magical question, "And what else?"

Often these simple questions lead to a 20-minute near-monologue by the client, interrupted by only a few questions from me, at the end of which the client has got clarity, or even resolved, an important issue that was staring them in the face. The key is to listen for the whispers: What is below the radar screen of the client that might be essential for their future? One client had given a presentation to his superiors in London that, despite his fantastic product idea, had got a surprisingly lukewarm reception, and had left him with a sense of unease. In the normal course of events he would have brushed it off and continued with his business as usual. My question, "What's on your mind?" eventually brought up this unease, so we debriefed the presentation carefully and found that he had not prepared the presentation with his audience and their interests in mind. When we prepared his next presentation, in Denver, we applied the lessons learned. The client told me later that this had been the best presentation he had ever given, with people emailing him for weeks afterwards with enthusiastic feedback and ideas. At the source of his accomplishment had been simply my listening for an opening for coaching.

If for any reason the opening did not occur in the player's first monologue, you can ask the follow-up question, "And what else?" and at least one opening for coaching is bound to arise in the answer to that question. Watch for certain words that stick out in the player's tale. In my coaching, there are usually several openings and then the player can say which one (if any) they want to work on.

It's not only what the player says, it could be how they sit in the chair, how their eyes wander, what they do with their arms. What is their body language, their facial language, the sound of their voice? Albert Mehrabian, a professor emeritus at the University of California Los Angeles (UCLA) did one of the very few quantitative studies of communication. He found, in essence, that only seven percent of communication happens through the words, the other 93 percent is something else. That something else is the tone of voice (38 percent) or the body language and mimics (55 percent). All these dimensions have an impact on communication and according to Mehrabian, they account for 93 percent of the communication. So, even what you are reading in this book right now is only seven percent words and there can be a lot of misunderstanding because you don't hear the inflection of my voice, you don't see my body language, you don't see my mimics, so you might miss out on irony or tongue-in-cheek statements.

That's probably why George Bernard Shaw, the early twentieth-century British playwright, once said in desperation: "The biggest problem about communication is the illusion that we have accomplished it."

That's why there are so many misunderstandings between men and women, between colleagues and between nations and cultures.

And that's why it is extremely important that you watch and listen for all the signals coming your way because the raw material and the opening for coaching could be hidden in any of them and not just in the words the person is saying.

Big Data
But, come to think of it, the process of revealing openings for

coaching starts before your first conversation with the player. As the coach, you are on high alert. You are like a camera that records massive amounts of information. When I walked into the building to meet my player for our very first meeting, I took note of everything. Nothing was irrelevant. The way the receptionist greeted me downstairs—in her own way she reigned over the company, she knew everyone and everything, and I noticed that you had to stay on her good side or she would discard you to a nowhere of inconsequence. Or I watched how the top manager I was going to work with treated the receptionist. That could become raw material for the coaching. It could even be how the office is constructed. I try to see what is the culture in that organization, what is the culture, the environment surrounding my player. Basically anything around that person can reveal the context in which the player speaks and lives. What is not said? What is in the background or in the periphery? Everything that people don't even see anymore because it is always around, like the wallpaper, so people take it for granted and don't question it anymore.

I took note of the way the senior executive offices on the third floor were constructed—the corridor around the building was incredibly and eerily quiet, all the doors to the various offices were closed, and on the corridor you couldn't hear a peep from the offices. So I immediately made a mental note: "Little or no communication here? Steep hierarchy?" The highly functional interior design without any fluff, interrupted by boring art on the walls, if any, and the absence of any personal gadgets in the offices were other symbols I could use to decode the prevailing culture.

You take mental notes about everything. Later on you might discard some of these mental notes, but others will become central to your coaching process.

CHAPTER 6. QUICK WIN I: GET A PLAYER (= CLIENT)

> *There are at least two kinds of games.*
> *One could be called finite, the other infinite.*
> *A finite game is played for the purpose of winning,*
> *an infinite game for the purpose of continuing the play.*
> *The rules of the finite game may not change;*
> *the rules of an infinite game must change.*
> *Finite players play within boundaries;*
> *infinite players play with boundaries.*
> *Finite players are serious;*
> *infinite games are playful.*
> *A finite player plays to be powerful;*
> *an infinite player plays with strength.*
> *Finite games can be played within an infinite game,*
> *but an infinite game cannot be played within a finite game.*
> *A finite player consumes time;*
> *an infinite player generates time.*
> *The finite player aims for eternal life;*
> *the infinite player aims for eternal birth.*
> —James P. Carse, *Finite and Infinite Games*

Does everybody need coaching? My answer is no; people don't *need* coaching, it's not as if they'll die without it. But everybody benefits; everybody could use coaching. To take myself as an example: I am successful (though it's not the custom to say this out loud in Switzerland). Nonetheless I am grateful for coaching in almost every domain of my life. Whether it's on my investments, on real estate, on business or on writing, I have the benefit of a different coach or sparring partner in each of these domains. (On family matters or major life decisions, I use my best friend or my psychoanalyst as a coach.) Do I *need* them? No. For example, I didn't have access to my psychoanalyst while he took a year-long sabbatical. I was completely okay without him. In fact, sometimes I channeled him silently: "What would Dr. X say right now if I told him about his issue?" and I was able to come up with some ideas. And one of my best friends, who happens to be the godmother of our younger daughter, is at times a highly useful coach in almost any area of life. It's not that I *need* these coaches, but coaching has truly elevated my performance.

Does Roger Federer need a coach? Not really, he could probably perform quite well without a coach but his performance goes through the roof with the coach. That obviously happens when you have a really good coach. At the end of reading this book, it is my intention that you will be a great coach as well.

This chapter teaches you how to get a player (or if you prefer, a client). It's simple, but not easy. By now, you are clear that you could coach anybody; that almost any occurrence, from a complaint to a success to a performance review to an open issue to a promotion, presents an opening for coaching. You know that the coaching relationship is very different from any other relationship. You know what coaching is not, and you know what coaching is. Now it's actually time to get a client, no matter whether or not you are a professional coach or wanting to be a professional coach. You might be a manager in a company or an officer in the military; you might work or volunteer at an NGO or in a school, in a religious institution or at the UN. You might be a parent who wants to coach her or his children. So, it could be anywhere in your life that you want to get a "client." I am using the word "client" interchangeably with "coachee" or "player."

Remember, the player is the boss, you are not their boss. Even if you are the player's superior at work or their parent in life, you cannot simply tell them what to do. (Well, you can, but it has unwelcome side-effects.) That is not coaching, it would mean using force and we ruled that out. There are several simple steps I want to guide you through. It is very simple—not easy but simple—to get a client.

Listing Prospective Players
The first step is that you list a bunch of people, I would say between three and ten. It could be anyone in your environment. It could be your teenage daughter who is in danger of using drugs. It could be a direct report of yours, a team member who is not quite performing o maybe they are performing really well and you want them to reach the next level of leadership. Remember, you could coach subordinates, you could coach sideways (somebody on the same level of authority as yourself), and you could coach somebody above you, even your boss. You might not choose your superior as your first coachee, which is a little bit more advanced, but if you want to, be my guest.

The point is; you can coach in all directions. You could coach up and down and sideways in your organization. You could coach your parent, your children, your spouse, your life partner. So just take a moment and list those three to ten people, people you care about, people you interact with often, people with whom you want a relationship in the future—not people you don't care about. Take a minute and do that. Once you've made that list, put three columns to the right of the names.

Player	Achievement / Strength / Asset	Gap	Next Level
A			
B			
C			
D			

The second column is, for each of these people, what are

their accomplishments, strengths, or assets. There are certain things each of them brings to the party that you can appreciate about them. Just put down some ideas; if nothing comes up that you can appreciate about them, fine, don't get stuck but. This person has produced breakthroughs in innovation or new technologies. They have built a beautiful family, they are an interesting conversation partner, they are mysterious and/or cool. Just put that for every name. What are some accomplishments or strengths or assets they bring to the party?

The next column to the right is, What are key gaps in their leadership, management or performance? It could be something that bothers you. What is missing? What's missing is not the same as what's terrible or what sucks or what's bad. What's missing is really another way of saying, what's possible. What's a gap? Again, if nothing comes to mind, just let it be, you don't need to know right now. It might very well be that you'll find out in your first conversation with the player. It's just a bit of homework before you go up to the person and ask, "Would you be open to coaching?" A gap in this person's performance might be that they are not quite reliable, they commit to an action and then don't deliver the action. There are integrity issues, they don't make their word count. When they make an appointment, they don't show up and the customer gets upset or feels as if they don't care. Another gap could be that the don't believe in their own leadership, thy don't have confidence that they can lead, maybe they keep themselves small. It works especially well to ask this question along the Global Leader Pyramid®: Gaps can exist at the level of Self-Awareness, Relationship, Vision, Strategy and/or Action.

The final column to the right is, What's their next level of leadership and/or management? What's their next level of development for a certain future, for the company's vision, for the strategy? Their next level could be, for example, that they take on the whole of China, they take on marketing or they become a reliable salesperson who meets a certain target. It could be that they become a team player with a service mentality, they stop their habitual complaining and become more appreciative of other people.

Again, don't get stuck here if the ideas don't come immediately. Just write down what comes up, then let it go and move on to the next person or the next column. You should now have populated all four columns: The first, the names; the second, the assets; the third, the gaps or what's missing and the last, the next level for the future.

I assume you are doing this exercise. In my experience, people who skip over assignments like this rarely integrate their newfound insights into their practice. Remember, you want a new level in your impact and performance, your freedom and your peace of mind. If you want to be a masterful coach, you actually have to do these assignments. Nobody ever became a great coach by reading a book. You have to do the work. There is no magic elevator that gets you from zero to floor 100. You have to go through the trials and tribulations of the action. I can't control you, and since I am not your boss, I am not going to police you or manage you, it's really up to you whether you make that choice. But I'm confident that you do want to become a masterful coach, that's why you made the investment to get this book and you make the investment to spend the time. Obviously you would want a return on that investment.

Carving Out the Time
Once you have made the list, the second step is to make the time and that's actually not a small issue. I think all of us are close to the limit; our schedules are completely full with demands, with meetings, with things to do. It's typical of leaders that they have more on their plate than they could possibly manage. We don't really have time lying fallow for this new dimension of coaching, we need to make the time and make this a priority. But you might think it's much faster if you do it yourself instead of having to baby-sit people and hold their hands. You might think it's a lot more efficient if you just get the job done yourself and stop

wasting time on other people who might not perform anyway. And in the short term you might be right. In the short term, it might be more efficient for you to keep the task away from them and do it yourself. Then you know it's done right, quickly and along your standards.

However, in the long run, that's a disastrous policy because every time you take something away from somebody else, they will see that you can do it, so why should they? The next time they will say, "I don't need to do it because X is going to save the day again. If I wait long enough and don't do it, or if I fall short of doing it, X will take care of it, it's her problem" or "he is the leader." More often than not, people tend to make themselves small, to reduce their commitment, to shirk responsibility.

So coaching someone means making an investment of valuable time. It might take a few minutes longer in the short run, but in the long run the investment will pay off. The ROI will be their leadership, their initiative, their ownership, their responsibility and/or their commitment. In turn this will free you up to move on to other things. So in the long run, coaching is a great investment to make but you have to want to make the front-end investment.

Carve out the time. If necessary, create a timeslot in your calendar. Say on Friday morning from 10am to 12pm, you make time for coaching people; or if you prefer, you could block out 15-30 minutes each day FOR a coaching conversation with at least one person.

You need not coach all of the people on your list—at least not right away. That might be too ambitious at the beginning. Don't bite off more than you can chew. You might select three of them and start with those. If you are really completely under the water, select just one person.

Whomever you selected, be sure you have their best at heart and are willing to put aside your judgments and filters or whatever else you may think about this person. See if you can truly say, "I'm willing to commit myself 100 percent to that person's success." (You don't have to like the person to make that commitment.)

Scheduling the First Conversation

The next step is to schedule at least one conversation with that person. Ideally you would schedule several conversations but the person probably doesn't even know yet that you want to coach them. So you set up the first conversation with the person and you might say, "Listen, do you have time? I would like to talk to you about something. Let's go into the conference room," or you might say, "Are you up for lunch?" Make sure the message does not come across menacing in any way. You could say, "I'd love to discuss something with you—a new possibility." Hopefully they say yes; if they say no, don't try to convince them. If they don't even have time for lunch, you simply approach another person. Most people will say, "Sure thing, I've got five minutes." You might want to respond that the minimum for this conversation should be fifteen minutes.

In the last chapter we talked about creating the opening for coaching. But that's only the beginning. You need to create demand; then you need to set the ground rules; and even though it may not be a written contract, you need to build an agreement so that you each know the ground rules and you know what you can count on each other for. All this is ultimately about trust.

Building Demand for Coaching

The first step in the conversation is to build demand for coaching. Remember, coaching without demand is mere noise, it's a mere interruption or disturbance in the player's life, or they will likely think, "Why are you wasting my time, taking me away from my work?" So you've got to build the demand for coaching.

And how do you build demand? The key is enrollment: The player has to sign on by choice. The coaching has to be on their own purpose line. You know by now that you cannot im-

iCoach

pose coaching; coaching has to be something the player wants. So you have to be clear on their concerns, their wants, their fears. Can you have the possibility of coaching show up on the player's agenda? Even before you meet with the player, you can stand in their shoes, in their world, and anticipate, given your knowledge of them and their enterprise, what might be their possible concerns. To place yourself in their world, you might have to do your homework. As you Google them and/or their enterprise, you can write down some intelligent questions that will show them that you have their concerns at heart.

Then, at the first meeting (or, as the case may be, on your first call or Skype) you can ask those questions. We already talked about "What's on your mind? How are you doing? What issues are you facing? What keeps you up at night?" You might say, "In all the accomplishments I have been able to achieve in my life, I always had a sparring partner, a confidant by my side. I would love to do that with you as well. That doesn't mean I'm better than you. I'm offering you conversations that might expand your impact or your performance. Are you open to that? Are you open for coaching?"

Sometimes you might need to talk about your credibility. Why do you have credibility? "I accomplished X; I opened the market in India and I think I can help you think through what that would mean for China." By the way, with my daughters, I constantly have to build demand for coaching. I have a core value that I don't want to manage our kids, I want to coach them so that they become who they can be rather than me controlling them. So I have to build their demand. Sometimes you can do it by saying, "I've been there. I have accomplished something similar. I have faced an issue similar to the one you are facing now. Would you be open to exploring some options about this?" You might establish credibility by saying, "I have worked with dozens of people and they used me as a coach to achieve a performance breakthrough. Would you be interested in that?"

And what can you say if you don't have any results under your belt? What can you do if you have never coached anybody and you can't really build credibility that way? If you revisit your life biography, you see that the great things you have accomplished, anything significant you and/or people around you have accomplished, probably required you to work with other people and assist them in the achievement. Maybe there are those who have never supported anybody in achieving anything. But if you look at your life long enough, you will see how you supported others in their success. For example, outside my professional life I was a ski instructor at the age of 17 to 19 in Davos and I had this class of 30 boys that were completely wild and crazy. All they wanted was to go straight down the hill, and I was scared to death that one of them would break a leg. That was my first leadership experience, to herd those cats and help them come down the mountain safely. Looking back, it was coaching.

At the age of 20, I worked in the theater and directed an adaptation of Shakespeare's "Romeo and Juliet" with teenagers. Looking back, working with those kids was coaching too. Then, at the age of 22 I joined an international NGO at the UN and had to empower 27 global affiliates to produce breakthroughs in performance. We ended up producing a 45 percent annual compound increase in revenues while keeping expenses stable.

My assertion is that you have had similar experiences in your life where you can say with confidence and integrity: "I have worked with X people and have had conversations with them that made them blossom and succeed, and I can do that for you too."

Setting the Ground Rules

You may want to make it clear that "Even if you say yes, you can cancel at any time because you are the client and can cancel the conversation and tell me simply, 'Listen, this does not empower me anymore. Thank you very much but o don't think this is useful.' No questions asked, no hard feelings. You can stop anytime."

There are other ground rules; one is that the player is the

boss. "I am not your manager, I am not your policeman. I am not going to hunt you down, this is not another trick to get you to do what *I* want. It is really me being your thinking partner, a sparring partner, a confidant to assist you with whatever conversation you need to be great, to go to the next level."

Another ground rule, essential to this confidant relationship, is confidentiality. "All of our conversations would be absolutely confidential. They stay solely between you and me. I would not talk to any other colleagues, I would not talk to your or my boss about it. This is absolutely off the books, off the record. What happens in Vegas stays in Vegas."

You want to build a safe space with the player. Let them know that nothing is taboo. "There is nothing outside of the scope of our conversations per se. If by any chance a drinking problem or a problem at home has an impact on your performance, that becomes crucial to the conversation. If you are willing to trust me and to share that with me, I am happy to have it in the conversation and I will keep it 100 percent confidential. You have my word, I will never ever use anything you say against you and I will never disclose it." That's very important. "There is also nothing you could say that is stupid. If you have a thought, feel free to express it so that you can see what it sounds like and once it is outside your mouth with your sparring partner who is 100 percent committed to your success, then you can see whether or not you want to act on it."

Another ground rule is that the client has to initiate any coaching conversations. The coach usually does not initiate any conversation. The client does; he or she requests coaching. You tell the player, "Again, this gives you the initiative and responsibility, but also the control as my client. The client is king. In this relationship, you don't have to report to me in any way. If you don't come to me, I will assume that things are going fantastic and you don't need anything."

The final ground rule is that both player and coach honor their word. "When you make a promise, you either keep that promise or you honor your word by simply saying, 'I revoke my promise.' You don't need to give reasons. If you undertake an action commitment, you honor your word. The same goes for me as your coach, if I promise or request something and you say yes; or if you request something and I say yes, I will honor my word, which means I would either keep my word or I will let you know that I cannot keep my word, period. That way, we have a clean relationship.

There is a lot more to say about coaching relationships but that comes in *iCoach3*. This I think is all you need for now to have this initial conversation and to actually get your first client, and hopefully several. We did not talk about paying clients, which comes below. With paying clients, you have to jump one or two extra hurdles but nothing fancy. For now, whether or not you get a paying client doesn't matter. These are the first steps that you have to take to build a first coaching conversation.

Freedom of Choice
Now the player is ready to commit—but before that, I usually ask, "Do you have any doubts or any reservations about what we are about to undertake?" I got this question from Peter Block, a brilliant man and the author of Flawless Consulting, a book I recommend to any coach. He always asks the client to express any doubts or reservations. The funny things is, it sounds like a negative question. You are both inspired and want to get going, the player just wants to move forward and now you say, "Do you have any doubts or any reservations?" It sounds quite pessimistic, no? But unless the player can express their doubts, reservations or concerns, their commitment will be too shallow for the journey you both wish to undertake.

Another way of saying this is; if you can't say no, then your yes will not be powerful. I give you an example. I have told you about one of my favorite clients ever, he served as president for the European subsidiary of a first tier global energy company. I called him from my office in New York City as his chauffeur drove him in his Mercedes limousine from Hamburg to Munich at about 300 kilometers per hour, and introduced myself. His superiors at headquarters in Houston had leaned on him to get coaching. This was someone who did not really believe in coaching himself but he was willing to talk to me, basically to get headquarters off his back. There had likely even been an implicit threat: "If you don't take this coaching, then we would take that as a message that you are really not coachable and you are not willing to improve and we are going to fire you." That was kind of in the background.

And now the president and I were on the phone as his Mercedes was speeding on the German Autobahn, and I told him about the coaching process. Then he said: "I am not into this kind of Southern Baptist bullshit. I am not into vomiting my feelings." I told him, "Sir, that's not what this is about. What I am hoping to accomplish is that we can step back from the action and reflect on the bigger picture. And by the way, I'm not out to fix you. You are perfect the way you are. There is no expectation that you need to improve or be corrected. I don't do remedial coaching."

That put him at ease a bit. Then I said, "None of what I do has anything to do with what you call 'vomiting your feelings' or 'Southern Baptist bullshit'. It's really designed to step back from the action and reflect together. Sometimes, it's good to have a thinking partner, confidant who is from outside of the system but is a 100 percent committed to your success and not the handmaiden of senior management."

That was the bull's eye. It sold him. But it's not just what I said. But The point is that without the invitation to express his doubts or reservations, I would not have been able to have him sign on to the coaching process.

There could be other doubts, reservations or objections like, "I don't really have time for this. How much time would this take?" That's a fairly easy one. You could say, "I know your time is valuable. Mine too. We would work together about two hours per month. Can invest that much time to cause the sustainable change you want?" A bigger objection could be the one the president above had in the background. He didn't state this objection explicitly, but it was in the subtext. Without using those words, he told me between the lines: "I'm hostage to my boss in Houston. I'm kind of a prisoner. I have to get coaching because they told me get it."

This concern came up explicitly, and forcefully, from another client, a managing director at a global bank. She came into my office and basically said, "I can't really trust you. How do I know that you were not sent by my boss to fix me or change me?" I said, "My number one loyalty is always to the individual client. It's never to the corporation that hires me. Even if that cooperation pays my bills. I am telling the corporation that my first commitment is to the coachee." That goes a long way to building trust.

Now your player is—hopefully—ready to start. How do you design the coaching conversations? That's what the next chapter will cover.

CHAPTER 7. MIND SHIFT: LIFE AS CONVERSATIONS

*I have no theory. I only show something. I show reality...
I take those who listen to me by the hand
and lead them to the window.
I push open the window and point outside. –
I have no theory, but I lead a conversation.*
—Martin Buber

Let's do a little thought experiment. Imagine your child comes to your office and watches you work for a day. (If you don't have children, just take a colleague's child with you, the effect is the same.) What would the child say you do? Probably something like this: You are in meetings with other people. You are on the phone. You are intensely staring at a screen. You are typing on a keyboard. You are sending messages on your smartphone.

What is the common denominator of all these activities?

Your child sees you communicating. Consider that you are actually paid for having conversations. Everything you do, all day long, is speak and listen. When you review a spreadsheet on your PC, one could say you are still communicating, in the sense of receiving and sending information. (This sentence, as you read this book, is a message you're receiving from me.) Even when you take an action, that is a conversation. If you take the parking spot of someone else or honk your horn if they took your space, you are making a statement. If you hug someone, that is a form of speech. When soldiers walk in goose-step, they convey a message of order, hierarchy, and power. If you don't call someone back or ignore their email, you are sending a message. If you leave the office early, people receive a message, intended or not. If you look at a pretty co-worker, or a handsome one, you're sending a message; if you avert your gaze, you're sending another message.

The ground rule is, as the communication theorist Paul Watzlawick put it, You cannot not communicate.

What Is Peugeot—Really?

My brother-in-law works for Peugeot/Citroën. I'm not sure if he would agree with what I'm about to say here: Peugeot is not made up of its cars, its offices, its money or even its people. Yuval Noah Harari, in his book *Sapiens*, shows how you could take all that away and Peugeot would still be Peugeot:

> In what sense can we say that Peugeot SA (the company's official name) exists? There are many Peugeot vehicles, but these are obviously not the company. Even if every Peugeot in the world were simultaneously junked and sold for scrap metal, Peugeot SA would not disappear. It would continue to manufacture new cars and issue its annual report. The company owns factories, machinery and showrooms, and employs mechanics, accountants and secretaries, but all these together do not comprise Peugeot. A disaster might kill every single one of Peugeot's employees, and go on to destroy all of its assembly lines and executive offices. Even then, the company could borrow money, hire new employees, build new factories and buy new machinery. Peugeot has managers and shareholders, but neither do they constitute the company. All the managers could be dismissed and all its shares sold, but the company itself would remain intact. It doesn't mean that Peugeot SA is invulnerable or immortal. If a judge were to mandate the dissolution of the company, its factories would remain standing and its workers, accountants, managers and shareholders would continue to live – but Peugeot SA would immediately vanish. In short, Peugeot SA seems to have no essential connection to the physical world. Does it really exist? Peugeot is a figment of our collective imagination. Lawyers call this a 'legal fiction'. It can't be pointed at; it is not a physical object. But it exists as a legal entity. Just like you or me, it is bound by the laws of the countries in which it operates. It can open a bank account and own property. It pays taxes, and it can be sued and even prosecuted separately from any of the people who own or work for it. Peugeot belongs to a particular

genre of legal fictions called 'limited liability companies'. The idea behind such companies is among humanity's most ingenious inventions.[33]

Organizations as Networks of Conversations

Decades before Harari, in the 1990s, theorists questioned the picture of the organization as a stable entity. Strategy experts C.K. Prahalad and Gary Hamel, for example, described corporations as structured around core competencies, avoiding rigid or permanent structures and instead developing a capacity to respond with great flexibility to external and internal change. Skills, tasks, teams, and projects emerge in response to a need; when the need changes, so does the organizational structure.[34]

"But an organization can only exist in such a fluid fashion," wrote Margaret Wheatley already then, "if it has access to new information, both about external factors and internal resources. It must constantly process this data with high levels of self-awareness, plentiful sensing devices, and a strong capacity for reflection. Combing through this constantly changing information, the organization can determine what choices are available, and what resources to rally in response. This is very different from the more traditional response to information, where priority is given to maintaining existing operating forms and information is made to fit the structure so that little change is required."[35]

I am going further. Consider that Peugeot, or your company—indeed, any organization—is, in essence, a network of conversations. It is what people (managers, workers, board members, customers, and society at large) say it is. It is what people hear when they hear the name "Peugeot."

Benny, my brother-in-law, would probably say I'm nuts. And I'm not saying this view of organizations as spaghetti of conversations is the truth. It's not true. It's what my colleague Jay Greenspan used to call an "empowering lie." But it might be a useful model of reality—especially for coaching. Bear with me as I show you how.

If we assume that everything in life is conversation, that

life is made up of conversations, that's an eminently useful model of reality. If things in life are not fixed, not static, not permanent, but essentially language, then we can change them, mold them, shape them. Why? Because all human beings, regardless of how much money they have, how much authority they have, what job title they have, whether they sit in the corner office or not—they all have the power to speak and listen.

People usually think of conversations as hot air. We tend to take conversations for granted because they have always been around, from the day of our birth. So we are a bit careless with what comes out of our mouth and what goes into our ears.

But conversations are far from trivial. They can build up or destroy. You can kill someone with words—well, perhaps not physically, but you can kill them off in terms of their leadership, their initiative, their motivation. You can kill them even by how you listen to them—or not. Ignoring someone is a surefire way of killing them off.

By the way, conversations need not be only what is spoken or listened to. Albert Mehrabian, professor emeritus at UCLA, found that only seven percent of communication is the words. 55 percent are the context in which the communication happens (the simple word "Yes" can mean very different things when said in Brazil or in the Netherlands) and the tone of voice ("I love you" can sound sincere or sarcastic). 38 percent of the meaning in any message are carried through the body language and the mimics. (That's why, by the way, it's usually disastrous to want to resolve a conflict or tell a joke via email or WhatsApp: Since written communications don't allow you to see or hear the speaker, much of the meaning is literally lost in translation.)

Leaders Manage Conversations

Are there productive and unproductive conversations? How can we tell the difference between them? And: Are your conversations effective? Can you eliminate those conversations that are ineffective or irrelevant or even destructive? How can you manage your conversations such that they match the outcomes you want?

I assert that the conversations that take place inside the "box" determine how the box works. I assert that whenever you fail, that failure is merely a symptom of some conversation going wrong. And whenever you succeed, it means that you had a series of conversations that led to success.

Life is made up of conversations—this is not the truth, but an empowering model—and the role of the coach is to manage a distinct set of conversations. And conversations are not one big soup, despite the fact that they sometimes seem that way. In the next chapter we will see what types of conversations there are so you can manage them systematically.

CHAPTER 8. FRAMEWORK: FIVE STEPS TO POWER & IMPACT

*All models are wrong,
but some are useful.*
—George Box

If life consists of conversations, then logically, coaching takes place in one or several conversations. The following distinctions come from James Flaherty who wrote one of the seminal books on coaching. It's called *Coaching* (surprise)*: Evoking Excellence in Others.* His book is consistent with my coaching philosophy.

The ***single conversation*** is the first type. A player comes and tells you, "I need some coaching" or you offer coaching, for example to prepare for a certain assignment; or they might have a presentation next Thursday. You ask the player, "Do you want to go over it together?" This is single-issue coaching: The player wants to resolve a specific issue or think through a single task with a sparring partner.

A single conversation could also serve to sharpen a particular skill, it could be that the player says, "I noticed I don't listen well, I don't have a repertoire of listening. Can we have a conversation about building that skill?" Or you might offer a conversation to build a skill, it could be that the player is at a loss to deal with politics in the company, so you could have a conversation to look at how to act as a political animal because politics is not really their thing. "I just want to do my stuff," they might say, "but I noticed that politics gets in the way". So you might have a single conversation to sharpen a specific skill, like a strategy skill, communication skill or self-awareness skill.

Often coaching is of the second type, the **multi-session coaching** that goes over multiple conversations but it's still designed to break through vis-à-vis a particular issue. Let's say the player has a toxic boss and needs to find a way to build an effective working relationship with him or her. It could be that they get resistance from their team to their vision and/or strategy. The player wants to see how to work through this, making sure that people get on board and maximize the alignment and buy-in. So that could be done in a multi-session coaching.

Flaherty calls the third type of coaching a **long conversation**, which could last over multiple sessions or really half a year or a full year. The player and you take the space and time to have a long extended conversation. Its purpose would be to cause a fundamental change.

For example, with one client, the CEO of a multi-billion-Euro company of 12,000+ employees, we worked for three years to move the company from A to B. The company was quite engineering-driven, ridden by clashes between the older and younger generations, and reactive. My client wanted to make it more proactive and lead it to the digital future of home automation, artificial intelligence, blockchain and other new technologies. Such a fundamental change requires a long extended conversation over time. The same goes for a fundamental change in the player's world view or performance. For example, if a client at a global bank wants to move from being Director of the IT Centers of Excellence to being the CIO and a managing director, a strategy for such a move might take six to 12 months to come to fruition.

Say a player has a major business imperative or a major

personal imperative in their career they want to meet. Masterful coaches have masterful conversations. How do you manage masterful conversations that result in your player achieving his or her desired future? In the last four decades, I have developed and refined a simple but powerful framework for managing masterful conversations.

The Global Leader Pyramid®
Basically, you could frame the coaching process—indeed, any major accomplishment you wish to build—as a five-level pyramid: Self-Awareness, Relationship, Vision, Strategy and Action (see Fig. 1). I (and thousands of clients, students and readers) have found that when you want to—or have to—build an accomplishment, be it big—like building a satellite for the European Space Agency ESA—or small—like a successful meeting with the boss—the most effective pathway is to work through these five levels and to move to the next level only once the previous level is complete. Inversely, if something is not working or if there is any breakdown, the Global Leader Pyramid® serves as a diagnostic tool to see where to focus the troubleshooting.

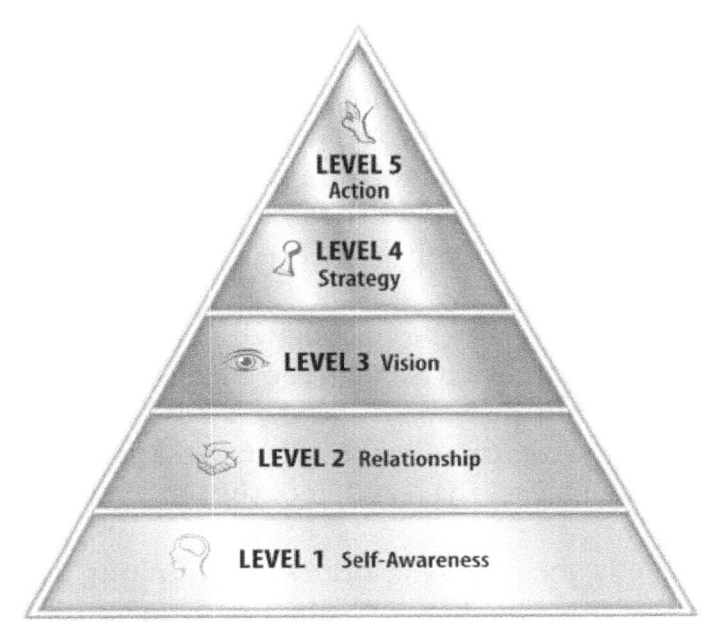

Fig.1: The Global Leader Pyramid®

    On the ground floor of **Self-Awareness**, you observe yourself constantly to make sure that you, as your own coaching instrument, are tuned finely enough to make great music with the client—just like a guitarist or violinist who tunes his or her instrument before they start playing. I found out the hard way what fiascos happen if you fail to do this fundamental step and fly blind instead. Great havoc has been wrought by leaders who were unaware of the hidden motives underlying their actions. At this level you check your own assumptions and blind-spots, you examine your culture. You ask "Why?" (for example, Why am I impatient, Why am I angry or sad, Why is this important to me?).

    When ventures go awry, it is rarely because of technical factors. What gets in the way all too often are sub-conscious ra-odblocks like ego or pride, greed or fear, survival or self-preservation. A key derailer are blind spots and flawed assumptions. As Mark Twain put it, "What gets us into trouble is not what we don't know. It's what we know for sure that just ain't so."

It would be a good idea to assume that you and I are pretty much blind. Daniel Simons coined the term "Inattentional (or Selective) Blindness." You may have seen the video where two teams toss a basketball back and forth in front of an elevator, and your job as the viewer is to count the times the ball changes hands. Most people count correctly: fourteen times.[36]

But did you see the gorilla?

Most likely, at least on the first viewing, you did not. Which is logical, since our brain is much too small for processing all the visual stimuli that come its way. So the brain has to prioritize: It emphasizes only a small part of what comes in through the eyes, and ignores the rest. Hence the term Selective Blindness.

The problem is, most of what drives our opinions, decisions, behaviors, actions, and hence results lies in an invisible, sub-conscious domain. It's like an iceberg: More than 90 percent lies underwater. All too often, humans (and yes, even managers who pride themselves of being "rational" and "objective") fall prey to cognitive fallacies.

On the ground floor of Self-Awareness, you answer the question, "Why?" For example, Why is this important to me (which reveals my values and/or interests)? The "this" could refer to a key decision, or a standard operating procedure, or simply an agreement like starting a meeting on time. Why am I getting impatient or angry or depressed (or any other emotions I might be feeling)? What are my (personal or cultural) blindspots or biases in looking at this issue? At this basic level, you check your own assumptions and make sure you are looking at the evidence, rather than through some filter of a past-based prejudice. In short, fact-based, not fiction-based.

On the second level, **Relationship**, you build a partnership with your client that is strong enough to withstand the inevitable challenges of climbing a mountain together. Unless you go at it alone—which, if you work with another person, is impossible by definition—the gear is not enough. You need trust; you need to know each other's values; you need to be clear on your commitment to each other; you need to clarify your mutual interests and expectations. And when I say "the client," I do not mean the organization that hired you; I mean the player you are coaching. The fundamental question you ask at this level is "Who?" (for example, Who are you, Who are we?).

When the legendary football coach George Allen was fired on Christmas Day 1968, a year after he had shared the title of NFL Coach of the Year with Don Shula of the Baltimore Colts, his players stood by him. A few days after the shocking announcement that Allen was out of a job, twelve Rams players held a press conference, beseeching management to reinstate their coach. "We won't play," his players said, "if George won't coach." Allen stood beside his men, dark sunglasses covering his eyes.[37]

The third level is **Vision**, where you basically ask a very simple question: "What?" (for example, What do you want, What do we want?) You assist the player in building a future that inspires them, that gets them out of bed in the morning, that is truly their own. You also ensure that they make room for that future to live in their present, and that their actions reflect that future in the day-to-day. You ensure that they stand in that future (this might well be the most important role of the coach, being committed to the player's commitments). And you ensure that when the future gets lost in the onslaught of daily activities and demands, the player can bring it back.

The fourth level is **Strategy**. Here you ask what it will take to achieve the vision. The basic question at this level is "How?" (for example, How will we do this, How can we ensure success)? What are the resources needed? What could go wrong?" Strategy, in this framework, is simply a bridge between Vision and Action. This is where you make sure there is a roadmap for realizing the future. You do this by confronting that the player has only 24 hours each day, that his or her resources are limited, and that the fulfillment of his or her commitments happens within (or despite) those constraints. So, as strategy guru Michael Porter put it, "The essence of strategy is choosing what not to do." So you have to say No, set priorities, and postpone or delegate or nix low-leverage or irrelevant actions.

Finally, the penthouse suite of the Global Leader Pyramid® is **Action**. Without action, nothing would ever happen. At this level, you make promises and requests. You ensure that the actions are a match for the Vision and Strategy. You build visual displays that pull for enough of the right actions. And you declare breakdowns if there are barriers or blockages in the way of performance.

Just as coaching consists of conversations, each level of the Global Leader Pyramid® consists of effective conversations at each level. Self-Awareness is not a mysterious or psychological mental state but a conversation: You have a conversation for Self-Awareness (mostly with yourself, as a self-reflection, but perhaps in a second step also with the player), asking yourself, Why does this matter to me? Trust, shared interests and shared values are the result of a conversation for Relationship. Inspiration, commitment, alignment and a future-based mindset arise in a conversation for Vision, as when John F. Kennedy declared, "It should be possible, by the end of the decade, to land a man on the moon and bring him back to Earth safely." Planning, feasibility and clear priorities emerge from a conversation for Strategy where you analyze the current situation vis-à-vis the Vision and ask, among other questions, What's missing? What are the blockages? What are the opportunities? and then build a "reverse roadmap" from the future back to now. And actions and results are catalyzed by a conversation for Action—for example through a promise or request, an offer or invitation, or through declaring a breakdown ("What we are currently doing is not a match for the opportunity" or "This costs too much—what are you going to do about it?") as a call to action.

Of course this short overview is merely like the menu in a restaurant—reading what's on the menu is nothing like actually eating the steak. Similarly, the pithy descriptions above fall far short of doing justice to each level of the Global Leader

Pyramid®. Learning to master the distinctions and tools at each level takes a lot of work and practice. (Disclosure: I have been at this for close to four decades and am still working on some of these distinctions.)

Bonus: The Coach's Self-Assessment
In this spirit, I have prepared a special, free self-diagnostic tool for you. The Coach's Self-Assessment systematically follows the five levels of the Global Leader Pyramid®. It's simple: Under each of the five levels, in each skillset, you rate yourself from 1 (i.e. terrible, you suck at this) to 5 (masterful, you can call this forth in another person). This diagnostic will allow you to map out your own development plan for building key coaching skills—as you see fit.

I put the Coach's Self-Assessment tool online, for two reasons: First, I update the self-assessment periodically. Second, even if you are reading the paperback version of this book, you can print out the self-diagnostic as many times as you see fit. Get your free Coach's Self-Assessment here: https://www.leaders-academy.online/icoach1-bonus1

More about each level, and the highest-leverage coaching tools at each level, is covered in detail in the other books of this series; *iCoach 2* will teach you the art and science of decoding hidden motivations (your own and, afterwards, those of your clients)—perhaps *the* foundational skill in coaching and leading. *iCoach 3* will show you how to build a powerful coaching relationship and how to position yourself as a sparring partner whom the player surrenders to. In *iCoach 4* you will learn how to build a compelling future with the player. *iCoach 5* is about how to assist the player in building a dynamic strategy and shoring it up against all eventualities. And finally, *iCoach 6* will give you all a fool-proof methodology for actions, results and making the player unstoppable.

For now, a gentle reminder: Comedian Jerry Seinfeld said once that the challenge of being funny never lets up. No matter how funny you were five minutes ago, the audience is unforgiving. Five minutes of bad jokes, and you've lost them.[38] Being a coach is very similar to being a comedian in this respect: You don't have the luxury of a bad move. The client is constantly watching and evaluating whether the interactions with you are worth his or her while—after all, they are paying you with both money and time. One bad interaction and your coaching relationship is in jeopardy. But no pressure ;-)

CHAPTER 9. SIX KEY COACHING QUESTIONS

When will the rhetorical questions end?
—George Carlin

Once upon a time, a man found a cocoon for a butterfly, with a small opening. He sat and watched the butterfly for what seemed like hours as it struggled to force its body through the little hole. After a while, it seemed to stop making any progress. It appeared stuck.

The man decided to help the butterfly. With a pair of scissors he cut open the cocoon. The butterfly emerged easily, but something was strange. Its body was swollen and its wings shriveled. The man kept watching the butterfly, expecting it to take on its correct proportions. But nothing changed. The butterfly stayed the same. It never flew.

In his kindness and haste, the man had not realized that the butterfly's struggle to get through the small opening of the cocoon was nature's way of forcing fluid from the body of the butterfly into its wings so that it would be ready for flight.

Like the sapling that grows strong from being buffeted by the wind, in life we all need to struggle sometimes. It makes us strong. Likewise, when we coach others, it is helpful to recognize when people need to do things for themselves.[39]

Advocacy or Inquiry? The Power of Questions
The key method for letting people do things for themselves is

to ask questions—and then, if I may be so blunt, to shut up and listen. Good coaches listen more than they talk. Sam Rayburn, the former Speaker of the U.S. House of Representatives, put it this way: "No one has a finer command of language than the person who keeps his mouth shut." At the opposite end of the political spectrum, the actress Vanessa Redgrave, a Maoist, put it in different words: "Ask the right questions if you're going to find the right answers."

The neuroscientist Jeffrey Schwartz found that the right question holds profound power: "The questions you ask of your brain significantly affect the quality of the connections it makes, and profoundly alters the patterns and timings of the connections the brain generates in each fraction of a second."[40] The right question can alter the focus of the brain: "Focus your attention on something new, and you make new connections. This has shown to be true through studies of neuro-plasticity, where focused attention plays a critical role in creating physical changes in the brain... If you pay enough attention to a certain set of brain connections, it keeps this relevant circuitry stable, open and dynamically alive, enabling it to eventually becoming (*sic*) a part of the brain's hard wiring." Schwartz has shown that people can do this themselves, through what he calls

> self-directed neuroplasticity, or the ability of an individual to alter his or her own brain activity through the active practice of focusing attention in constructive ways. Perhaps the classic demonstration of this was in people suffering from OCD, who with just a few weeks training, and a lot of effort, were able to systematically alter the brain circuitry underlying the intrusive 'something is wrong' thoughts and urges with which the brain bombards people suffering from OCD.[41]

If people suffering from obsessive-compulsive disorders can change their brain circuits, then do you think you and I can do it too as we face down our demons? Yes we can, you bet we can. It's a no-brainer (forgive the pun). By contrast, when you give answers, the brain stays within its existing patterns; the status quo prevails; no innovation happens.

The problem is that you and I (especially, but not only, the men among us) are hard-wired for advocacy, for persuading or convincing people of whatever opinions we hold dear, or at least of offering well-meaning advice. Even if you mask your advocacy by asking a rhetorical question like, "Could you do X?" or "Have you ever thought about Y?" that is still tantamount to giving advice. And remember: Advice (at least advice without demand) is noise in their ears. As my colleague Michael Bungay Stanier puts it succinctly, and with a bluntness that Swiss neutrality and diplomacy simply do not allow: "Stop offering up advice with a question mark attached."[42]

Asking an open-ended question yields far more leverage. Usually open-ended questions start with a W, such as "What would that mean to you?" or "Why does that rile you up?" or "Who can do something about this?"

Good coaches never quite tell you what to do. They resist giving you the answer. They allow you to find your own answers.

I cannot overstate the importance of shutting down your "advice monster," as my colleague Michael Bungay Stanier calls it, your advice machine because then you fall back into this trap of knowing better than the player. Worse, the pitfall is that you're using them for *your* agenda. The key difference of coaching is obviously that it's about *their* agenda, not about using them for what you want. It's about finding out what they want and then helping them get there. Of course there has to be an overlap between what they want and the business imperatives of the whole company.

The Bare Bones of Coaching: 6 Key Questions

Now we're ready to delve into the action; after all, it's called Coaching-In-Action. There are six key questions you can ask in just about any coaching conversation, no matter what else you talk about:

- ☐ What's on your mind?

- ☐ And what else?
- ☐ What do you want?
- ☐ What are your results?
- ☐ What's missing?
- ☐ What's next?

By the way, you don't always have to ask each of these questions. If you harbor by any chance a reservation that coaching takes too long, let me assure you: You can coach in ten minutes or less. It doesn't have to be a long conversation. True, there has to be a sense of space and safety necessary for a shared inquiry. You cannot just coach between the door and the desk, but you can coach in very little time—as long as you stand firmly in the principle that coaching is not top-down exploitation but shared exploration.

Question 1: "What's On Your Mind?"
The first question, "What's on your mind?" is a pretty great question. Why? It's not a small-talk question like "How are you?" If I ask you, "How are you?" then the answer is likely "I'm okay, thanks," which might shut down the conversation. On the other hand, neither is it such a dramatic question that the other person would feel button-holed, like "What has kept you up at night? What gives you sleepless nights? What is *the* major problem you're working on?" Such questions might be too intrusive for a first question. "What's on your mind?" is a nice middle ground between those two extremes. And this is not just because I'm Swiss and we like neutrality. "What's on your mind?" works well in any culture.

Now this is important (and at the risk of repeating myself): After asking this starting question, *shut up*. Don't talk while they're talking. This is of course easier said than done; take the medical profession. In 1984, Harvard did a study of doctor-patient communication. The patient comes into the doctor's office and the doctor says, "What happened? What's bothering you?" and the patient starts talking. Then the doctor interrupts the patient. On the average, after 18 seconds. We've all been there: You walk into a doctor's office, and the doctor asks, "What brings you here today?" You start to answer. Eighteen seconds later, the doctor interrupts you mid-sentence. The study found that fewer than two percent of patients got to finish their explanations. When Dr. Wendy Levinson, vice chairwoman of the University of Toronto's department of medicine, studied malpractice suits, she found that bad communication is a common theme. What often prompts people to sue their doctors, Dr. Levinson said, "is the feeling that they were not listened to, that they didn't have the doctor's full attention."[43] Problem physicians come in many guises, patients say: the arrogant or dismissive doctor, the impatient doctor with his hand on the doorknob, and the doctor who is callous and judgmental.

Ideally, doctors would have "a combination of the most technically sophisticated skills and knowledge and the best communication skills," Dr. Levinson said, "because that will get us the best outcomes from our patients."[44] Research has shown that good doctor-patient communication resulted in lower blood sugar levels in diabetic patients, and lower blood pressure in hypertensive patients. Other studies have found connections between positive patient-physician encounters and the reduction of pain in cancer patients, improved physical health in people with various illnesses, reduced stress and anxiety, and better adherence to prescribed treatments.

Patients don't even need face time with doctors to experience positive results. Researchers discovered that phone calls from nurses or other clinic staff members to provide emotional support go a long way to help people quit smoking, stay on medication, or shake low moods. In a large-scale, 18-month study, doctors in Seattle found they could significantly improve recovery rates for patients taking antidepressants by providing a few 30- to 40-minute counseling sessions over the phone.

Now the researchers held some unusual trainings: They taught doctors to shut up. (With all due respect to the demigods in white coats, that's no small feat.) Instead of saying whatever brilliant thoughts came to their minds, the doctors were trained to simply say "Aha". A patient would come in and say, "I've had some chest pain, I don't know what is going on." And the doctor just said, "Aha."

Into the short silence, the patient said, "Come to think of it, my brother had a heart attack a few months ago." And the doctor said again, "Aha". So after a few sentences, the patient had pretty much self-diagnosed.

(My experience with clients has been analogous: If I asked a good question and then kept my mouth shut, the client usually provided valuable intelligence and virtually dictated to me the diagnosis, the intervention needed and even the contract terms. All I had to do was listen and take notes.)

Did these findings and trainings change doctors' practice? Fifteen years later, a follow-up to the earlier study found that now doctors no longer interrupted their patients at 18 seconds—now it was after 23 seconds, a five-second improvement in fifteen years.[45]

(If you think bad listening is limited to the medical profession, think again. Managers are not one iota better. They might actually be worse. I'm not aware of studies on how quickly mangers interrupt colleagues or customers, but it would be surprising if it were after more than 18 seconds.) That's the first question: "What's on your mind?" And then shut up.

Question 2: And What Else?
The second question is, "And what else?" (Frankly it's another way of saying, "Aha.") "And what else?" is an important and powerful question. It sounds like nothing, but "And what else?" opens up a whole new dimension. The player might not have thought about something, or they might not have thought it important enough to share with you. You'll be amazed at what this simple follow-up question reveals if you just listen. In essence, the question "And what else?" is a strategic question.

Obviously, I can interrupt more quickly but usually,

when I ask them that and they have space to express whatever is on their mind, without censorship or taboo and with nothing out of scope, they might come up with insights they didn't consider before but that are essential to bring up.

Question 3: What Do You (Really) Want?
"What do you want?" This question can take many guises. It could be, Where do you want to be in five years? Or I ask a variation thereof, "Where do you want the company to be in 5 years?" It depends on whom you are coaching. If I am coaching one of my daughters, I would probably say, "What do you want to be when you grow up?" Or you could ask, "What's your company's vision? The question "What do you want?" targets the person's vision, as long as they don't fall prey to self-censorship. Sometimes I ask, "What are you fundamental life commitments?" That's another way of asking, "What do you want?"

Usually, when the player says what they want, then I ask: "What would that mean to you? What's the significance?" For instance, if a says, "I want to be executive vice president," then I ask, "What would that mean to you if you were executive vice president of the company?" Or I could ask, "How did you get to be executive vice president?" In other words, "What value did you add to the company or to its customers that would qualify you in everybody's eyes to be executive vice president?" To dig deeper, you can follow up that question. They goal is that the player express why this vision matters to them and why they want it. What are their values underneath? What are their commitments underneath? All of this goes under the umbrella of "What do you want?" as the third question.

Question 4: What Are Your Results?
The fourth question is so basic as to sound trivial: "What results have you achieved toward your vision? What outcomes have you had?" This question is designed to bring back reality and pinpoint performance. Another way of asking the question would be, "What outcomes have you had since we last talked?"

Results can be either quantitative or qualitative. It might be that the player has produced a new $250,000 client contract, or a new relationship that might give them access to the Chinese market, or they might have had an insight. "I had this realization, 'Wow! All my life I have been spending on proving X."

Alternatively you could ask, "What is the status of your objectives?" The status can be, one, it's complete already, an unlikely case; two, it's on track; three it's behind; four, it's in danger; or five, it's abandoned.

The basic idea of the question, "Your outcomes / status?" is that the coach creates a tension between where the player wants to be in the future and where they are right now. That's the tension, the gap in which you stand with them. As a coach, you serve as advocate of the player's commitments and future, but you cannot discard the present, or it would be like dreaming. Of course nothing is wrong with dreams; for example, dreaming of a world that works for everyone, a world free from hunger, a world where everyone has enough money is wonderful, but unless there is a relationship with the current reality right now, dreaming doesn't move the needle. As a coach, your main job is to serve as the bridge-builder between the player's desired future and the player's "now." The question, "What are your results?" really builds that bridge—or at least it opens up the gap.

Question 5: What's Missing?

"What's missing?" is one of the most magical questions I ever learned to ask in my career as a coach. If I could ask one question only, it would be this one. If in your coaching you did nothing other than asking, "What's missing?" by that question alone you would add major value to your players' lives and works. If you only have five or ten minutes, you can simply ask, "What's missing for success?" The player might say, "I'm in X project, we want to bring this solution to market, we want to build this prototype, we want $10 million sales in Singapore." The question, "What's missing?" immediately shines a laser light on the player's focus? We don't need to focus on everything that's going fantastic. The previous question— What are your results? —already did that. The player can and should acknowledge, appreciate, recognize and take stock of what they have. But "What's missing?" takes the player into the tension between the present and the future of filling the gap.

"What's missing?" can take many guises. You can ask, "What exactly is the challenge here? What are the obstacles? What are the opportunities?" Note that "What's missing?' is fundamentally different from "What's wrong?" "What's missing?' is not "Who's to blame?" "What's missing?" does not pull for complaints. "What's missing?" pulls for something possible, but hidden, not yet seen, not yet revealed. "What's missing?" is a future-based question, while "What 's wrong?" is a past-based question. "What's missing?" is designed to reveal a new opening for the future. It serves simply to bridge a gulf between the player and the result, or between the player and the future.

Question 6: What's Next?
The sixth question, "What's next?" is again a deceptively simple one. Sometimes, if a player and I are engaged in multiple coaching sessions, toward the end of a meeting I usually ask first: "When would you like to meet again? What's a good rhythm that would make sense? Do you want to do in in six weeks, in two weeks, or in a month?" It's useful, but not imperative, to schedule the next session by the end of each session. You could leave it open and up to the player (as long as you can live with the uncertainty and the risk that coaching will go out of the window for the player).

One advantage of having a next scheduled session is that you could then ask, "What are your priority actions up to the next session? We are going to see each other again in X weeks. What are your major priorities by that time?" A variant of the question might be, "Based on our conversation today, what are the three major priorities you will focus on?"

Make sure that the player phrases each of those priorities

with a clear—and ideally measurable—deliverable. "I'm going to talk to some people" or "I'm going to make some calls" or "I'll call clients" are not acceptable statements of priorities. They are too vague and not specific enough. To deserve the name "priority" or even better "promise," each declaration must have a clear outcome, a deadline, and measurability so that that you can either quantify or at least verify whether the player delivered or not. (Imagine winning a tennis or football match without keeping score on a board.) Either you did meet with the board and got alignment on X decision or Y policy, or you did not meet with the board at all, or you met with the board and didn't achieve alignment. The outcome should be as specific as possible. The more specific their promise is, the more likely the player will succeed. (If you don't like sports, take apartment hunting: Unless you say exactly what you're looking for, including the bay window and the fireplace and the pricing, you'll pretty much leave it to chance whether you'll find the place you want.)

"What's next?" is really a conversation for action and needless to say, it's all about action. The entire process is called "Coaching-In-Action." We're not talking merely about great insights or mental breakthroughs; those breakthroughs and insights must lead to performance, to a change, to a result.

At the risk of sounding like a broken record, this need not take a lot of time. It does not have to be an endless discussion. The player can produce major changes this way based on the simple question "What's next?"

Listening *To* vs. Listening *For*

And again, your listening is paramount. My late mother once asked my father: "Heinz, aren't you cold?" As in any statement, there were three subtexts. First, self-disclosure: "I'm cold." Second, a request in hiding: "I'd like you to close the window or bring me a sweater." And third, a positioning in the relationship: "As my husband, you're supposed to take care of me." As a husband, and even more so as a coach, it's crucial not only to listen *to* what people are saying to you but to listen *for* the subtext underneath the iceberg. Listen for the hidden meaning, listen for what the player is saying and may not even be aware of saying it.

For example, you might stop the action and say, "Interesting. Did you notice that you used the words 'I must go to work'? What does the word 'must' mean to you?" One word created a prison for them; the subtext might be, "I'm forced to go to work, I'm a slave, I'm a prisoner, I'm a hostage to the senior management."

Now I might sound like a hair-splitting anal Swiss, but listen to your player as if every detail counted. Listen as if every word that comes out of the player's mouth hid a subtext that might reveal their mindset, and your job is to read between the lines. Every word the player utters is potential raw material for coaching. If you can listen for where they might be in a prison and they don't even know it or where they might unwittingly shoot themselves in the foot, that's where the real value of your coaching comes into play, since habitually they would push that thought aside and say, "I don't have time for this and need to move on. I got more important things to do." But it's often in those details that you unearth a major new opening.

The Only Way to Fail Is Not to Play
To sum up this chapter: The key questions to ask are very simple, you can do it probably under fifteen minutes or maybe even under ten. Now the question is: How do you extricate yourself? The title of the next chapter is "Exit Strategy—Fire yourself." Before we go there, one remark: You might say some stupid things—and so what? It's not the end of the world. You might ask a stupid question; or perhaps you discover a question that works even better than the six questions above. The only way I could find this out was by actually doing it and messing up 50,000 times and becoming pretty masterful through my mess-ups.

The great thing is, while you're in training (and you always are), and yes, even while you make mistakes, you can still add value. The only way to fail at this would be not to do it at all. So I encourage you to get out there—as Nike would put it, just do it—and test this methodology in the action.

CHAPTER 10. EXIT STRATEGY: FIRE YOURSELF

Come to the edge, she said.
They said: We are afraid.
Come to the edge, she said.
They came.
She pushed them...
and they flew.
—Guillaume Apollinaire

Let's say you have been in the action coaching and experimenting with the six magical questions from the previous chapter. You've given your player valuable insight and helped them develop their own solutions. Now the player went for it, took action—and promptly forgot that it was actually the conversation with you that revealed the solution. We've all been there: The player thinks they did it themselves. They boast about the brilliant idea they came up with. And they give you zero credit. (And if the player happens to be your boss, this can be quite annoying; imagine your boss saying at the next staff meeting: "I've been doing some thinking, and I had this fantastic idea...")

Here are several answers to this. First, zero credit is actually a good thing—it means you're a masterful leader. I'd like to quote the saying by the ancient Chinese sage Lao Tzu over 2,500 years ago (it's the motto of this book and well worth repeating here):

> *As for the best leaders, the people do not notice their existence.*
> *The next best leaders, the people admire.*
> *The next, the people fear, and the next the people hate.*
> *But when the best leader's work is done,*
> *the people say "we did it ourselves."*

Second, if somebody comes up with a solution that you helped them reveal and bring to life, and they go for it and then forget where it came from, they might have forgotten on the surface, but underneath they remember. Something reminds them, and they will want to work with you the next time around—and it will probably make your next coaching conversation easier since the demand is already there. Even if the player forgets to credit where it belongs—to you—they will likely end up with a stronger demand for your next coaching.

Third, the player gets to step back from the action, they get to reflect, they get to consider all the options, they get to see things in a new way. That's a huge added value even if they are not fully conscious of it. Even if they sucked that up because it is so rare, they will likely come back for more the next time around and see you as a source of the solution eventually.

The fourth answer is that the value-add of coaching is self-evident. The very fact that the player has built his or her own solution *is* the added value. If you had given advice, the solution would be extrinsic, which means the player might like it, they might even say, "That's good advice" but it's not theirs since they didn't come up with it. By contrast, when you coach in a spirit of inquiry, in an exploration (not exploitation), then the solution is intrinsic: The player will come up with their own solution, which makes the arrived-at pathway much more actionable because they came up with it, they own it. The pathway is also much more sustainable. You don't have to follow up and say, "I'm the policeman, I have to manage and monitor you and make sure you do this," which would be all extrinsic. The powerful thing about coaching is that it is intrinsic.

Finally, and related to the fourth answer, the player will be more self-reliant because they came up with the solution themselves, so the next time they will likely be more capable to come up with their own solution, they will be more competent and more self-determined. They will also be less dependent on you. In other words, they will be more able, more of a leader.

You guessed it: Yes, you have to examine your own motives to see if the player's greater self-reliance would be truly okay with you. If you want them to depend on you or you want them to come back, that might be a problem that they are less dependent. This obviously requires some humility in your part and you should rejoice with them that they came up with their own solution and that you then have more space and more time to deal with other things because they won't need you anymore.

The Savior Syndrome
Therein also lies a value-add for you as the coach. Just in case you harbor a doubt or reservation that goes something like, "What do *I* get out of this? I might actually lose power because the player will go away and not need me anymore. And I can't be the hero / guru / savior (take your pick) anymore."

I encountered this "savior syndrome" (as I call it) in a large, multi-billion automotive supplier in Europe where the Executive Committee got much of their validation from being the company's heroes saving the day. A senior manager, for example the CFO, would come into the ExCom meeting and say while catching his breath, "I had a major crisis in the plant in Brazil, I had to fly there all the way from Paris and bail them out, it took me the whole week." They tell these hero stories, and they get tremendous acknowledgement and recognition from saving the day (in addition to more hidden payoffs such as looking good and busy in the eyes of their bosses, peers and teams; a sense of superiority; being right while making "those incompetent Brazilians" wrong; dominating regions in the company's periphery; escaping the domination of their own work at headquarters; and having a good excuse for not meeting their objectives on other fronts). At the same time, there is a huge cost in time, money and energy, not to speak of the health risks to the managers who are constantly on the verge of burnout. Worse, this savior behavior keeps the company's top and senior management in chronic crisis management mode. And worst of all, it's unsustainable: It does nothing to make that Brazilian plant more self-sufficient or self-determined.

Be vigilant against this hidden mindset of needing your player. If your player depends on you less or not at all, this is actually another value-add for you and ultimately for the entire organization. If people depend on you less, the organization depends on you less. That does not mean they'll fire you—on the contrary, you are then free to move to the next level of responsibility. You will go on to greener pastures yourself. At the same time, you build people power around you—not followers who would be mere slaves or tools for you, but leaders who think for themselves and act in the interest of the company.

More than that: If you do coaching right, you will be less overwhelmed, have a lot more freedom, and do more meaningful work. This goes for both of you, the player and you. When you step back and reflect, the bigger picture will emerge and a bigger meaning will emerge in your work and life, beyond merely getting hung up in surviving meetings or your job. That is a huge added value for both of you—the client and the coach.

Refuse to Help
There is a related pitfall here: People might come up to you and want to pull you into their stuff. They might even say they are open to coaching but what they really want is that they want you to do their work for them.

Once my friend and colleague Peter Block once told me in a workshop based on his book *Flawless Consulting*: "Refuse to help."

"What?" I said in disbelief. "Refuse to help? That's ridiculous. My whole life is about helping people." No. Refuse to help because helping people assumes that they are incapable of helping themselves. Helping assumes, with a patronizing whiff of arrogance, that you know better than others how to get what they need. Helping people keeps them small, helpless, dependent on you. (By the way, the entire existing paradigm of international aid, as the name says, is built on helping helpless people—with disastrous consequences such as a total lack of sustainability—but that would go beyond the scope of this book.) By saying, "I will help you, I will develop you". You put yourself on a higher level than the other person. That is not coaching; it is about correcting people. Although many so-called "coaches" offer "remedial coaching" to fix someone or knock them in shape, that does not deserve the name coaching. Coaching is not about me knowing and you not knowing. "You poor guy, you recipient of my assistance… I am going to show you how it works." That, I think, is the context in which Peter Block meant when he said, "Refuse to help."

True to this context, another colleague, Michael Bungay Stanier, wrote in his book *The Coaching Habit* what he calls "the lazy questions." Whenever people come to him for help and they basically want him to save them and take care of their work, he says, "You have to develop the ability to say yes more slowly." You may recall that I said somebody who always says yes is probably a pinball of circumstances and not a leader. An essential part of leading is knowing when to say No. You need to say No in an intelligent way, you cannot say it to abruptly, or you will not be seen as a team player. People will say, "This guy always says No. She is not on the team and we might want to get rid of her."

Michael calls it "Saying yes more slowly," which is a great way of saying it. He suggests six simple questions:
- "Why are you asking me?" Then see what they say.
- "Who else have you asked?" Is there anybody else who could do this?
- "When you say this is urgent, what do you mean?" What is your evidence for urgency? Why

is it urgent? Maybe it could be done next year.
- "According to what standards does this need to be completed and by when?" Find out exactly what needs to be accomplished.
- "If I couldn't do all of this; if I could do just a part of it, which part would you have me do?" What part you really cannot do or cannot find anybody else to do? Cut the demand down to size.
- "What do you want me to take off my plate in order to do this?" My plate is full. It puts them on notice that there would be an opportunity cost. If they ask you to do X, then you can't do Y.

These questions are designed to put the ball back in the player's court so that they don't fall into the trap of asking you to save the day, since that is not coaching. The player is the one responsible. Yes, the player is the boss, the player is the client, the player is right; but the privilege of being the boss comes with the responsibility that it is their accountability. It is not your job. So we close this chapter with this caveat so that even in the action, in the final steps of the coaching process, you keep yourself clean and squarely in the scope of the coach. Don't deviate from that.

Some people might try to manipulate you into helping them, but in my experience, most people who run into a wall see themselves genuinely as helpless. By asking these so-called lazy questions, you are actually empowering them in building self-reliance and resourcefulness. They discover that they can manage and find a way through without you having to save the day. More than anything else, that builds sustainability.

Earlier in the book, under what coaching is not, we covered different relationships people can have. We said clearly at the time that coaching is not helping, you are not just a friend, you are not a psychologist, and so on. This is just to remind you that at any time in the coaching, you may need to clarify the role of coach. The coach is not in the helping profession.

Bonus: The Coaching Debrief

I have prepared another free bonus for you that might come handy at this stage. This tool has often been useful to me—and to my clients—in stepping back at the conclusion of coaching, seeing what's missing and systematically coming up with what's next. I put the Coaching Debrief form online (a) so you can always get the latest, most up-to-date version, and (b) so you can use the Coaching Debrief with as many clients as needed. Go to your free Coaching Debrief here: https://www.leaders-academy.online/icoach1-bonus2

Now that you have learned how to fire yourself, as it were, from the coaching role, how do you ensure that the player will perform at the higher level of leadership and won't fall back into the past? In short, how do you ensure sustainability? The next chapter will give you a system for achieving sustainability. But before you go into that chapter, I recommend that you go out there and test these distinctions in the action. Observe what happens, and have fun.

CHAPTER 11. SUSTAINABILITY—7 DEBRIEF QUESTIONS

> *If you learn to listen,*
> *you will find that each life*
> *speaks to us of love.*
> *Because love is the key to everything,*
> *the engine of the world.*
> *Love is the secret energy*
> *behind every note I sing.*
> —Andrea Bocelli

This chapter is about sustainability: How can you sustain the momentum after the coaching—after your exit—because your mission as a coach is not only to be the advocate of the player's future and commitments, but also to build autonomy, or better, self-reliance?

Why self-reliance? You want to ensure that the player has built some competencies and can basically fly by him- or herself when you're not around anymore. As we saw already above, this presents you with a dilemma—it has been called the doctor-patient dilemma: On the one hand you want the patient to get better, to be healthy and fully vibrant. On the other hand you, like everyone else, need to make money, so you actually benefit from the patient *not* being well. This is a widespread dilemma in healthcare. As a coach, you have an obligation to make sure that people do not become dependent on you. You want to clarify for yourself: Are you really willing to let the player move on?

To be perfectly honest with you: In my own coaching practice, at times I had a hard time saying good-bye. I remember one client of mine, I have mentioned him before, the third-generation CEO of a family-owned company that had grown to €1.6 billion revenue.

Frankly, I tend to fall in love with all my clients. (And I'm in good company: The most successful sports coaches, from Red Auerbach to Pat Riley to Phil Jackson, said a key success factor in pulling for championship performance was their love for their players.[46]) Put more accurately: I don't love them personally—that's reserved for my wife and daughters—but rather, I love their commitments. So I fell in love with what this CEO was up to. He and I met about once a month in a hotel conference room in another city, secretly. Even his company's human resources department didn't know about our coaching sessions (except the HR chief, who knew only because he had signed the contract). We weighed strategic and tactical decision he had to make to prepare the company for the next decade and lead it there by empowering his management team and workforce. It was a fascinating assignment to be his confidant and sparring partner—his *éminence grise* in the background.

After three years of committed partnership, the time was ripe to move on. We both realized this. I was sad to let him go (as a client only—our friendship has remained). At the same time I noticed that my abiding mission in life had always been making people self-reliant. They should never depend on me. My mission as a coach is much more important than my feelings of attachment—and much more important than my desire to make money. And I'm always happy when people tell me, "I can now fly by myself," which again is consistent with the famous quote by Lao Tzu we already revisited above. "When the best leader's work is done, the people rejoice and say, 'We did it ourselves.'" That has to be the motto, the mantra that you imprint into your brain and into your heart.

Dr. Thomas D. Zweifel

The Road to Sustainability: 7 Questions
Let's go into seven systematic questions you can work through with the player at the end of a coaching assignment. Having distinguished three types of conversations above (single-session, multi-session and long conversation), let's assume you are now coming to the end of the conversation. If it's a single conversation, you might not need to do everything I'm saying here, or maybe nothing at all. If it's a multi-session or a long extended conversation, then you definitely want to go through these seven debrief questions.

Question 1: What did you accomplish?
The player's accomplishments through the coaching process would be both quantitative and qualitative results. They could include "I got a great R&D officer on board and put him on the executive committee"; or "I produced €5 million in additional revenue from new products not on the market when we began." Or it could be accomplishments like what the player learned. What did they start doing, or stop doing, or do differently since the start of the coaching? One client, the European president of a tier-one global energy company, told me: "I learned to go beyond the rules I had imposed upon myself."

Another way of asking this would be, "What struck you, what surprised you?" Yet another is, "What three key insights or realizations did you have?" The player might have gained certain insights, for example "I learned to step back from the action periodically, for self-reflection and strategic thinking."

An insight comes at times as a flash of inspiration. "Ah!" told me one client, CIO of a financial services provider, heading a 120-people team. "I discovered that I have spent my entire life trying to please other people." The insight was so powerful that it brought tears to his eyes as he said, "I have spent my entire life trying to find out what other people want and what they need, and giving it to them rather than doing what I want to do and need to do." That might sound like a trivial no-brainer to you, but to him it was a fundamental insight.

iCoach

Question 2: What did you not accomplish?
The player may have set certain objectives that they didn't meet. It's always good to acknowledge those. By the way, the question "What did you not accomplish?" can lead to a next coaching assignment. The player might say: "I also had an objective to improve my public presentations, to be a public speaker and to speak to the media without any fear, without clamming up. Why don't we have another bunch of conversations to build that skillset?"

The question puts integrity into the process, lest they player might harbor some unfulfilled expectations and, God forbid, might think the coaching wasn't all that useful. Your question puts these expectations on the table so you and the player can see what to do about them. "How do you want to still accomplish that objective that you didn't accomplish?" (Remember, I always say "you" here; yes, it is a partnership, but first and foremost it's the client's job to achieve their own objectives. The coach is only the facilitator.

Question 3: What worked?
This is the question about what tools in the coaching worked for the player that they want to use again, to sustain, or even to scale up and have their team get access to. Another way of asking the question is, "What was most useful or valuable to you?" The question could come even at the end of a single conversation. "What was most valuable, most useful, what did you discover here? What did you develop for yourself that is useful?" By useful, I mean it's not just a nice theory, but you can use it in the action and apply directly in your life or as a manager or leader.

Sometimes I suggest to the player to build a leadership display of all their team members. This spreadsheet looks a bit like the one you crafted (I hope) in the beginning of the book —remember? You listed the people you could coach and asked, "What did they accomplish? What's missing in their leadership and/or management? What's the intervention with each of them to provide what's missing? They might revisit such a leadership display regularly to see how to empower and/or develop their people.

One recent client told me, "This leadership display has worked well for me and I'll definitely maintain that." Another client might say, "What worked is to schedule strategy sessions with myself every Friday morning from 10am until 12pm. To take two hours out every week where I am just by myself, free to speculate about the future without any commitment to have to implement whatever I come up with. Just to dream, without obligation. That really worked for me." Yet another might say, "What worked for me was this business that we did on listening." Or, "What worked for me was to work on my own self-awareness and understand what drives me through life. I'll definitely keep exploring that because that gets me centered before I do my work." These are all examples of what actual clients told me when I asked them what had worked.

Like all debrief questions, "What worked?" is designed to build sustainability; once the player distinguishes a tool that worked for them, they're more likely to keep using that tool. If they forgot about a tool, or if it wasn't useful to them, they probably won't keep using that tool, in fact why should they? (By the way, for you as a coach: It works better to be quite unattached to all your brilliant tools in this conversation.)

Finally, you and the player may want to revisit certain principles that you revealed during the coaching process. A principle could be, for example: "I discovered the principle that it's always good to listen before I open my mouth." Or: "I discovered that when other people are upset, they're not necessarily responding to me." The principle would be, They're not responding to you. Or: "I discovered that if I'm too much for myself, I'm selfish but if I'm not for myself, then who will be for me? But if I'm only for myself, what am I? And if not now, when?" (That's a quote by the 2nd-century sage Hillel that I actually keep on my desk (as well as on my WhatsApp profile) as a reminder. That principle works for me—to always keep the balance between my self-interest and making a difference for others.) It's fun to reveal the ground rules the player intends to live by. They can then display those and keep them around themselves after the coaching.

You've probably noticed by now that I like quotes. A pithy quote can sometimes epitomize a principle powerfully and concisely. For example, Winston Churchill said, in one of the shortest speeches in the history of politics, to the assembled students in a school, "Never ever, ever, ever give up." (In fact the full quote is a bit longer: "Never give in—never, never, never, never, in nothing great or small, large or petty, never give in except to convictions of honour and good sense. Never yield to force; never yield to the apparently overwhelming might of the enemy." After these words, Churchill had to abruptly leave the stage to hurry to his war-room on 10 Downing Street.) That quote embodies a principle that a player may want to keep around. They can put it on their desk, in their smartphone or on a Post-It note on their desktop screen. This is just an example; you get the idea. What counts is of course not what works for you, but for the player.

Question 4: What Did not Work?
That gets us to the fourth question: "What did not work? Is there anything in this coaching process that did not work for you?" It clears the air when the player can say that something did not work for them. For example, the CEO above told me, "At one point, I asked you to write a brochure for me. You left the role of coach." He was right: After I had coached him on a speech outlining his vision for the company's future, he asked me to write a brochure for him. I drafted the brochure—and promptly got attached to my writing, while he didn't think it was all that great. That didn't work. Another example from a client: "It didn't work when you disclosed something we had discussed privately to our HR director." The question "What did

not work?" aims to put things on the table—and to leave nothing unsaid, nothing underneath the proverbial iceberg.

When the player declares what didn't work about the coaching process, one big pitfall is that the coach—you—start justifying and defending: "You didn't quite understand. I'll explain to you again why this is a great tool and you should use it." Defense and justification immediately have you fall back into the advice monster, where you are the one who knows and the player doesn't know. Remember, the client is the boss, you are not the boss, you are just a facilitator. That goes even for when you coach your direct report, even when you are the player's boss. When you wear the coaching hat, you are not their boss, they are the boss, and they have the sovereignty of interpretation. In other words, their interpretation is the valid one. Just as you would not tell a customer they are wrong, you would not tell the player he is wrong. The customer is always right; customer is king—and in our framework, player is king (or queen).

Speaking of queen: Do you know this one? You have a father; he becomes a father-in-law. You have a son; he becomes a son-in-law. You have a daughter; she becomes a daughter-in-law. You have a mother; she becomes a mother-in-law. You have a wife; what does she become? She *is* the law…

But seriously, "What did not work?" need not only be about the coach or the coaching. The question is also, "What did I discover that does not work in my life or work?" For example, "Working on weekends doesn't work and I'll stop that"; or "I discovered that it doesn't work when I always interrupt people. I tend to finish other people's sentences and I'll cut that out." The question calls not merely for the player to be a consumer ("I liked this, I didn't like that…") but to be a producer of their life and take responsibility for changing their future practices.

Question 5: What opportunities emerged?
This question points to a new opportunity, small or large, that revealed itself in the action and/or in your coaching. I would define an opportunity as an opening for action and a freedom

to be—it's irresistible, not just a possibility but an opportunity that calls you into action. For example, the opportunity could be, "I'll do more sports. I'll carve out at least one hour every two days for physical exercise." Or "I could present this new product, this prototype to the board of directors." Or "I could get the right stakeholders on board for a new project early on." Should the player decide to move to another country for their job, it is smart to get their family involved in the decision from the start. "Before this coaching I didn't think of that as possible and now, it's an opportunity I can act on."

Question 6: What leaders emerged?
Assuming the player leads other people (and remember, even parents lead their kids, so we are all leaders in some respect), you want to assist them in building leadership around them. The coaching enhances their co-leadership so other leaders emerge around them. Hence it is useful to take stock: "What leaders have shown up? How could you empower those leaders from now on? Do you want to acknowledge them for something they've accomplished? Do you want to coach them to achieve a goal?" Acknowledging and recognizing leaders who emerged during the coaching process, and seeing how to empower them, is crucial for sustaining the momentum.

Question 7: What's next?
Given the player's answers to all the questions above—What was accomplished? What was not accomplished? What worked? What did not work? What opportunities emerged? What leaders emerged?—the logical final question is "What's next?"

This is the question where the rubber meets the road. Here the player moves from reflection to action. The question can hold several sub-questions, for example: "If you could do three things differently from before, what will you do differently as a result of this coaching?" Or: "What can you see now as your next priorities?" Or: "Based on your answers to the six debrief questions, given everything you've said, building on what you learned, what do you see as your next action steps? What are your priorities for the next few weeks and/or months?"

Remember, you are letting the player go free now; but don't just abandon them. Make sure they have a plan or something to build. In a way, they are leaving the oasis and going into the desert. You want to be sure they have the equipment, they have enough water, to withstand whatever comes up as a challenge when they are back in the action flying solo. (Sorry for the mixed metaphors in the previous sentence. You know what I mean.)

Those are the seven debrief questions. Allow me a few reminders and comments. First, recall that all these questions are geared toward sustaining the momentum. You want the player to soar when you won't be around anymore.

Second, you need not ask all seven questions above. Of course ideally you would; but if you don't have time for asking all questions, you could simply start with, "What did you accomplish?", let the player answer that and then see what else they might want to unearth.

Third, these question apply whether you are coaching as a sparring partner from within the organization—a colleague, a team member, a peer or a superior—or as an external coach for somebody inside.

Now that you know how to build up the player's self-reliance, the next chapter will be about a special treat some of you might be interested in: How you can make money as a coach (only if you are so inclined of course).

CHAPTER 12. QUICK WIN III: MAKING MONEY AS A COACH (IF YOU WANT)

> *An egotist is a person of low taste—*
> *more interested in himself than in me.*
> —Ambrose Bierce

This is a chapter you don't need to read. Really. It is for those who want to offer coaching as a business. The chapter gives you turnkey tools I learned over time (I have been coaching for over 35 years now, made millions of dollars as a coach, and cut the tall grass since I started in the 1980s when coaching barely existed outside of sports). I went through my biography and recreated the steps I took and you can follow. Now of course every biography is unique; nevertheless, when I stripped away the idiosyncrasies, what appeared are a finite number of simple steps that make it feasible for you if you choose to have paying clients.

Action 1: Build Your Business Model
The very first question you have to ask yourself is: "What's my business model?" In other words, how will you make money? Most of us in the coaching or consulting profession are really in a business model called "pay-per-service." Usually the client pays per hour. (Since it is very hard to directly link business

outputs to coaching inputs, performance-based compensation is rare.) So we have a certain hourly compensation or daily compensation. One of my first coaching engagements was at a tier-one energy company in Hamburg, which meant I would fly from New York City to Hamburg and coach several top and senior executives in Hamburg, spending almost a full day (for example 10am to 4pm) with each player. More recently, when I coached the CEO of an electronics manufacturer, he and I met about every two months for about six hours. You can charge a certain amount of money for the time you spend.

But those were exceptions to the rule. Usually I meet people for two hours about every six weeks. That comes to twelve hours of coaching for the year or for the coaching engagement (and some coaches charge for the time they spend traveling to and from the client; I do not).

Remember, the client is the boss so they will determine how often it makes sense for them to meet with you. Some people need more frequent interaction, some people need more autonomy and independence and they will want it about every two months. I will definitely not recommend less frequently than every two months because you might lose the thread of the conversation.

The question you have to ask yourself to determine your business model is, "How much money do I want to make through coaching in a given year?" Say you want to make $120,000 or $200,000 or whatever the amount is you want to make in a year.

Next question: How many days of the year are you willing or able to work as a coach? Now, remember: You won't have billable hours only. You will have hours you spend on LinkedIn or marketing or sending emails to prospective clients or having conversations with them that are unpaid, not billable. You might still have another day job at the moment, you cannot yet put all your eggs into one basket. Or you might wish to coach at least one non-profit client where you work pro bono (I have done that to this day). Now the ratio is about fifty-fifty. Say you want to make $120,000 and plan to work 100 days. If you plan to spend 100 days on your new business, 50 of those days will be billable hours and the other 50 will be your current job, sales and marketing, billing and administration, and follow-up that is not billable.

What we are saying is you plan to make $120,000 in 50 days. Most of us need a calculator for this—I do, even though I'm a trained political economist: Making $120,000 divided by 50 means you would make $2,400 per day. Say a day has eight working hours, so $2,400 divided by 8 comes to an hourly coaching fee of $300 per hour. Such an hourly fee would be within the market in most industrialized countries. (In most emerging markets, the fees you can command are of course lower, but so is the cost of living.) For example, I work with a global bank. As an asset in their coaching pool, I have a framework contract with the bank so that I don't have to reinvent the wheel and create a new contract for very single coachee. It is clear to my partners at the bank that my fee is $500 per hour. And it is clear to me that for each of those hours, there is another hour I don't get paid for. So de facto, it really comes down to about $250 per hour.

If you have scruples charging such fees, consider two things: One, when I started out consulting, my then-business partner Erhard Bruderer insisted on charging $3,000 per day, which came to $375 an hour and seemed, to me at least, astronomical, obscene even. I had to do some work on my own mindset to get myself clear that my work was worth that much, and more (and it was).

Two, draw the client's attention—as well as your own—to the value-add of the coaching. When clients have considerations about high costs, I ask them, "What would have to be the outcomes of coaching that would make it a no-brainer to invest that much?"

Charging $300 per hour is fine, especially for executive coaching (there are other sorts of coaching where the fee might be lower). If such a fee is at the high end of your market, you might say, "I offer the Porsche of coaching." In other words, this will be luxury coaching.

Should you feel truly uncomfortable with charging $300 per hour, you can always choose another model; but then you have to adjust your business model. Something has to give. You might say, "I don't plan to make $120,000 but $60,000, so I will charge $150 hour."

But there are alternatives to simply lowering your fees (and it's usually better to compete on value than on price). When I charge a bit more, one little incentive I offer is this: "Listen, I'm not a bean-counter, I won't write down every single hour." I call it the Hotline between coaching sessions, whenever the client wants to get quick coaching on some issue they are facing. Say we meet once a month; after one week the client runs into a wall and needs a quick coaching. My line is open, they can call me, and we will either talk right then or we quickly schedule a call. It is a 10-15-minute conversation to clear up a single issue so they can be in action again. You can put this Hotline in the coaching contract so the client feels you are 100% committed to them (even if they never actually use the Hotline—and in my experience, many don't). They feel you care for them, you are available and they could make use of you any time (well, within reason—you could agree that they call you only during office hours). That way they don't have to wait until the next coaching session. The Hotline usually goes a long way to justify a higher coaching fee.

You can play with other value-adds too, depending on the assets you have to offer. Sometimes I offer clients to sit in on my leadership class at the university, and/or I offer them my books for free, which costs me under $100 for three or four of my books and $0 for shipping since I hand-deliver and sign the books—currently a $0 value but who knows? For the client (or the economic buyer at the client organization), it adds value because the books sustain the learning. They can go back to a book after the coaching engagement. You may want to look into your own life and see: Are they any things you can offer in addition to the pure coaching to kind of sweeten the deal?

Action 2: Generate Your Prospects

Once you have fixed your business model and feel good about it, the next task is to generate leads. List ten (10) people in your sphere of influence. It could be people whom you know, and who might benefit from coaching. It could be anybody whose business card or v-card you have. List people without censoring yourself—swing out. Virtually everybody can use coaching (take me: I've written books on coaching and yet I can profit from coaching too). There is nobody who will not perform at a higher level if they only had an external thinking partner, a confidant, a sparring partner with whom they can step back from the action, make sense of things, stand in the future, build compelling strategies, take decisive actions, all the while enjoying freedom to be themselves and peace of mind. There is nobody who doesn't want that.

So... Be generous. Who in your life? Could it be a peer in your company, or a team member, or a superior; or somebody outside the company whom you met at a conference; or a friend of yours, or someone else? Ten people should be the minimum. If you can list 20 or 100 people, even better, but start with ten people.

Action 3: Qualify Your Prospects

Next step: Qualify your prospect list. I usually evaluate my prospects along three criteria:

    A. Who "needs" coaching? "Need" is the wrong word. Who would benefit from coaching? Who would be empowered?

    B. Who sees you as a credible, value-add coach? Ideally, who thinks you walk on water—that you are a cool person to hang out with or that they could somehow benefit from conversations with you? Often these are friends, colleagues asking you for advice, acquaintances who come to you and like to talk with you.

C. Who has the budget for coaching? Ideally, the coachee and the economic buyer (the person who speaks the budget and signs the dotted line) are one and the same person, for example if your prospect is a CEO or C-level executive, but often they are not; the user buyer is your prospective client and the economic buyer is the HR manager who needs to be convinced of the value-add too).

Now put an A and/or B and/or C next to each name on your list. There are people who need coaching but they don't have money to pay for it. There are people who have money to pay for it but they don't want it. There are people who have money to pay but they don't think you are a credible asset. Ideally, all three criteria would be met but they don't all have to be met. They serve as a filter on your generated prospects to determine whom you will talk to first.

Obviously you would talk first to those people who fulfill all three criteria; they want coaching, they see you as a credible value-add and they have the budget. But don't get hung up on this—you are welcome to talk to people that have fulfilled only one criteria. It is just a way to prioritize and rank order people along the three criteria. On the top of the list are people that meet all three, then come the people that fulfill only two and then the people that meet only one. Then you can still decide whether it is worth talking to them.

By the way, you might think you don't know who wants coaching (whether they say so or not), who says you are cool or you are a guru or who thinks you are a credible coach. Some of us are not used to seeing the signals. So how do you know? What are the signals that reveal that somebody has a need for coaching or thinks you are an credible resource? I have seen that people who are extroverted might have a harder time to pick up those signals. If you are somebody who is more withdrawn, more introverted, that might actually be an asset: You might see more clearly who wants something. You can observe people based on how they behave; you can detect those signals. If you don't know how to detect openings for coaching, we covered this above. If you skipped over that chapter, you may want to go re-read it and see the symptoms that tell you as a "doctor" that this person could use coaching or thinks you are a credible coach. It could simply be that somebody comes to you for advice or that they call you often. It could be that they look around and seem confused. I usually see it when I enter a room and people come up to me; I can tell whether they are open to me and see me as a value-add rather than as a nuisance, a disturbance or an obstacle. I can see it in their eyes, in their body language and/or in their mimics. Those are some of the non-verbal clues you can pick up.

Action 4: Build Demand
The next step: You talk to your top prospects. You either schedule a call, a coffee or a meeting. If needed, go back to the section above on how to build demand, to see how you can use a trigger for actually making the phone call. You can say for example, "I hear you have been promoted to a leadership level. Congratulations—that's really cool. The same thing happened to me years ago. Suddenly I found myself in charge of this whole team. Maybe I could assist in some way. Is there anything you might need now? How is it going?" or something to that effect.

In that conversation, your job is to build demand for coaching by creating a need or revealing a need. There might be what I call a presenting issue, which is the initial issue you picked up as an opening for coaching. Then you reveal the real need and the demand, which means they will tell you they need something. Unless they want or need something, there is no conversation.

You can also build demand by establishing your credibility. You say, "I have done this before. I already work with clients"—or "I don't have clients yet but I do this a lot with friends and colleagues. I assist them with getting what they want."

Action 5: Agree on the Contract

The next part—assuming your offer meets a demand—is to discuss the budget and other contractual conversations. This is about setting up ground rules, a bit like creating an agreement. "How often are we going to meet? What is it going to cost you? What are some ground rules of confidentiality and openness to coaching? You have to willing to take risks and not simply say, 'I'm good, I don't need this' but be open to being disrupted and try things you have never tried before, or think about things you have never considered before. You have to open yourself up emotionally." Open communication is a key ground rule.

Another critical ground rule: Both partners make the coaching relationship a top priority. For example, if the coach calls the player (or vice versa, if the player calls the coach), you both agree to respond to any communication—emails, calls, WhatsApp, whatever—within 24 hours. In other words, this is a top priority relationship. Priority means prior to anything else. I will respond to you prior to anybody else because you are the top priority. That also goes a long way to build trust and build credibility with the player because they know that you are really there for them and vice versa. You need to know that they make the coaching a top priority.

Another key ground rule, as we saw in that chapter above, is that the player has to initiate the conversation and come up with a request for coaching, rather than expecting the coach to manage them. The coach is not the manager or the policeman; the coach is a resource the client has to use or manage.

The final and perhaps most crucial ground rule—I have said this before—is to "honor your word as yourself. If you make a promise in this coaching relationship, you will either keep that promise or revoke that promise, or change that promise, but honor your word at all times. You cannot always *keep* your word but you can always *honor* your word. The same goes for requests: If you make a request of me, I will either accept it, decline it, or counter offer, but when I accept your request or counter offer, then that becomes my promise and you need to be able to count on that. You and I need to be able to count 100 percent on each other.

"That's mutual accountability. The picture I always keep in mind: If I'm an acrobat in the circus and I jump off the trapeze, I need to be 100 percent certain that you'll catch me, and you need to be 100 percent certain that I am going to catch you." Or, if you prefer, take a military analogy: "If we are in war, I need to know that you have my back and you need to know that I have your back. Whether you serve in the police, as a fireman or a firewoman, it doesn't matter."

Those ground rules have worked for my coaching relationships. In the conversation, you might discover some other things that secure a powerful relationship between the player and you. For this kind of relationship it is irrelevant whether you like each other or have spent a lot of time with them. It needs to be a relationship that produces performance breakthroughs. If you don't have that relationship, then you cannot really go to work with the player.

I said in one of the last chapters. I would end the contractual conversation by asking whether the player harbors any doubts or reservations so that you can understand any concerns they might have. However you address these concerns, they either go into the contract or not. But they need to be on the table and be resolved so that there is nothing unsaid and the coaching is a totally open field. That is the conversation for the contract and the ground rules.

One footnote here: I have sometimes started coaching for free and told people, "I am not in a hurry. We don't need to immediately sit down and draw up a contract. I'm happy to meet a few times until I fully understand what's needed and what, if anything, we'll do together. Once I feel the need to be compensated, I'll let you know." Sometimes you can start coaching for free, but do put people on notice that you are usually not doing this. Usually you are compensated but you can start for free and actually build your credibility that way. They will see that you are providing tremendous value and then, if they have any honesty, it would be clear that this value-add should be somehow compensated. You can address that openly.

In my experience, sometimes it has been beneficial to start with just one or two conversations until we have really mapped out the player's current situation, where they want to be in five years, and what is missing for that. Between you and me, that is in fact a sales conversation, but you can frame it as a coaching conversation that you offer for free. Those initial conversations will give you the raw material you need in order to build the demand and then close the deal. To them it looks like free coaching sessions; to you, it is a sales conversation but one that adds great value.

One of the fundaments principles in my life is that in any interaction—even and especially in a sales conversation—I always provide more value than I ask for, so the client always walk out with a value-add from the interaction— whether or not they agreed to being a client. Even if I never see them again, they have received great value and they might talk to other people, and even if they don't, they are left with a great feeling about the interaction and about me. You often see each other twice in life. As the Australians like to put it: "Just remember that the toes on which you step today might very well be connected to the a__ you have to kiss tomorrow." That is an Australian joke, if you know the Australian culture, you will know that I mean. The more civilized way of saying it is that you always meet twice in life. What you sow, you shall reap.

Action 6: Your Online Bio

Now that we have almost come to the end of the chapter (and the book), there is one more action you can leverage. This action is not essential, it is a nice-to-have, but hey, you never know: I have made my LinkedIn profile my resume and rarely send out my resume anymore. If someone asks for my resume and they want it in a Word document, I still do that. But my resume is on my LinkedIn profile, which allows me to put multiple media: I have videos, I have book summaries, I have links to other activities, so people get a sense of the value I provide.

Since you are not me and I am not you, what you do is go back over your life and reframe your entire biography in the context of coaching. If you had to write your biography or resume, how would you talk about your life? You have probably coached people before, but it didn't have the label "coaching." You might have worked with your kids or spouse, you might have worked with colleagues or friends where you provided coaching, and only now, as you look back, it occurs to you that it was coaching.

For example, my earliest coaching experience was when I was a ski instructor in Davos. I was seventeen years old and had 30 kids under my command. Those kids, most of them boys, were skiing down the mountain like wildfire. I was praying that nobody would break a leg. If coaching means leading people to a desired result without sacrificing satisfaction or self-determination, that was my very first coaching experience: to lead them down the mountain safely, with maximum freedom.

Suddenly it occurred to me, "I was a coach already as a teenager." I had been a ski coach (if such a profession exists). Later on I became an actor, did theater animation with kids, and directed a play with teenagers, an adaptation of Shakespeare's "Romeo and Juliet." That was coaching too, even if it didn't look to me like coaching at the time.

Even later I worked for an international NGO at the United Nations. Again, I learnt coaching by working with 27 different affiliates and being accountable for their performance —without having authority to command or control. That was coaching pure. After leaving the organization, and having all this coaching experience under my belt, I built my consulting and coaching business.

I want you to look through your own life and see where you had an experience that could be reframed as a coaching experience. When you work in a corporate system or any organizational structure, you likely assist, empower or enable people to do something and co-lead with others on teams. You can put all those experiences into your biography. Then you may want to state them as coaching experiences on LinkedIn. You could ask people you worked with to post a recommendation on LinkedIn. At the least they can validate your skills: LinkedIn has a feature where you can click on certain skills on LinkedIn that you feel you are good at and then have people endorse those. (Connect to me on LinkedIn: https://www.linkedin.com/in/thomasdzweifel/ and see how I have worked "Skills & Endorsements" and "Recommendations.") Such marketing activity is unfortunately not paid, but it creates a background of credibility you can leverage in your coaching conversations.

We are at the end of the book now. I wish you a lot of success, a lot of clients, and a lot of money. May you make the difference you were born to make by working with other people. In my view, evoking greatness in another human being is one of the most exhilarating experiences in life. At least in my life, other than my family, this is one of my greatest joys—to see somebody go beyond themselves, embark on something they were dreaming of but never really considered possible, then achieve that; and to know that a series of conversations with me had an impact on their accomplishment. To see that I made a small contribution by posing the right questions, forcing them to confront a taboo, or asking them what was missing. To offer simple tools that helped them close the gap between their current reality and what they wanted. Assisting people in that way is a pure privilege and a major pleasure—and to be paid for it stretches credulity. If you are lucky enough to be paid for those conversations, it is the best of all worlds. To be paid for making a difference and to do what you love to do, that is luxury pure, and that can be your life. Now go forth and do it.

Dr. Thomas D. Zweifel

What Are You Gonna Do About It? Getting Into Action

The only thing standing between greatness and me, is me.
—Woody Allen

We have come a long way in this book. You now have a step-by-step turnkey system, a foolproof methodology that, assuming you apply it properly, will produce results—and now the time has come to apply it, to get into action. Specifically there are three things you can do now.

First, I find that if I keep insights in my head, they go away, since all conversations have a tendency to disappear. But when I articulate them in language, they become alive. (That is one of the reasons for writing my books.) Sharing my ideas with others makes them real for me. If I write my insights down and make them available to others, the act of articulation consolidates them. And it empowers others: They can then benefit from the best practices.

So the first action is: Share three key insights on Amazon.com that you got from reading this book. Share best practices that will be key success factors in your own coaching. You simply post a review and share your learnings (three bullet points suffice).

Second, let's face it: You are about to leave the oasis and go into the desert now. Make sure you have the equipment needed—and know what gear is missing or not impeccable. If for any reason you haven't done so already, fill out the Coach's Self-Assessment. Here the link again:
https://www.leaders-academy.online/icoach1-bonus1
The Self-Assessment serves as a diagnostic tool so you know your coaching competencies. What are your strengths and weaknesses? What are the areas you want to still develop in the action?

If you have the guts to do so, you may even want to ask

one of your coaching clients to assess you. Sometimes your self-view and the views on you by others don't match, so this might give you an additional reality check. This is of course your call.

Third, and most importantly, coach somebody. Go out and offer a conversation to someone. I cannot tell you how many times I've failed in my life, how many times I made mistakes, corrected and fine-tuned my approach. I kept looking what else I wanted to master, what else I needed to learn. There is nothing like action, action is the supreme virtue. The technology in this book has a potential million-dollar value, but only that: potential. None of it will make a shred of difference unless you apply it. So coach one person, have a conversation, fail, correct and then succeed. Don't be afraid of going out there and doing it. Once you do it, you will be great because intentions cannot be disrupted. If you keep the intention, there is no obstacle greater than your intention. As long as you don't give up (Winston Churchill's dictum: "Never ever ever give up…") you will be successful. As a coach, I don't tell people what to do, but in this case I'm telling you what to do: Don't do anything other than getting into action.

That is why this methodology is called "Coaching-In-Action." It is not called coaching in theory, it is not called coaching in the academy, it is not coaching in thinking. Get away from your desk, away from the office and into the field. I think you get the message, now you just need to do it. Close the book and do it.

THE ROAD TO MASTERY: THE ICOACH SERIES

This book was an introduction. You have passed several major checkpoints: Understanding the essence of coaching, what is not coaching, how to avoid the pitfalls. How do you actually see whether coaching is needed? How do you build demand? How do you build a powerful coaching relationship? What are the magic questions you ask as an effective coach? And how do you make money from coaching? I have sought to arm you with all the basic tools for basic coaching competence—and yet we have barely scratched the surface.

You might already know: The book you just finished (presumably) is the first of the *iCoach* series. Let me tell you about the others. Subsequent books in the series go much, much deeper, along the Global Leader Pyramid® that we covered above. I have poured each of the secrets I learned over 35+ years of coaching into each of these books. And just to be straightforward in this conversation: I am taking off my coach hat now and put on my marketing hat. My intention is, frankly, that you read another *iCoach* book, and ideally, the entire series. I venture to say you and your coaching prowess will benefit greatly.

iCoach2 will give you a building bloc that holds true power and can make you a masterful coach. This may sound a bit manipulative and even Machiavellian, but: How do you get into somebody's –anybody's—brain? The book will start with how you begin with yourself—as your own guinea pig—and decode the mysteries of the brain. We will see how you tick and what drives you through life. Where do you sabotage yourself, where do you shoot yourself in the foot (of course with the best of intentions)? Once you do that enough, you can do it with anybody. How do you get into the brain, into the mind? How do you reveal the types of games people play to get what they want (or think they want)? How do you unlock whatever needs to be unlocked?

My friend Michael Jascz calls it mind surgery. I am not sure I like the term, it sounds a bit violent and unilateral. But like a surgeon, you will go into the player's brain and find the levers that will allow them to make a major transformative shift in their life or in their work. As you know, it all starts with the mindset, it always starts with the brain. That is what brain science tells us. The book will go deep into neuroscience, using the latest findings from research and experiments. I have studied the science of cognition for the past several years and want to share what I have learned—in the context and service of coaching. Learn how to:

- Decode your own mindset and culture, see how you tick, and deepen your and your player's systematic self-reflection.
- Find the keys to unlocking the mind of any player, anytime, in any situation, and reveal the cognitive fallacies that trip up human beings—even the best of us.
- Get into the head of alpha animals (most often alpha males) and coach bosses up and down the hierarchy.
- Maximize your power in any conversation—not through force or authority, but through wielding the 5 types of power and expanding your repertoire.
- Be the wise guru who coaches your players through

tough ethical dilemmas—right-vs.-right decisions where the better solution is not apparent.

In *iCoach3* you will go deeply into the art and science of building, sustaining and deepening relationships. How do you build partnerships for life, partnerships robust and durable enough to withstand any of the winds of change? How do you build trust, that special something that has people flocking to you and follow your lead?

Perhaps *the* most important element in business and politics—not to speak of life—is trust. When trust breaks down, teams and organizations collapse, investors and customers go elsewhere, market value drops, mergers fail, people sue, even wars break out. How can managers build trust and credibility with their teams, peers and bosses? How can you position yourself as a trusted confidant—a *consigliere*—to the CEO, without being a yes-man? Based on over three decades as a CEO and coach to CEOs, I unpack the secrets of my high-performance relationships. I lay out the systematic steps of building and deepening powerful relationships—not through face-time, not based on alcohol, not even based on liking each other. You (and your players through you) will learn how to:

- Maximize your (and the player's) credibility and influence—not through fear or force or authority, but through building win-wins on shared values and interests.
- Decode the early-warning signs of an eroding relationship, and how you can rebuild and sustain the trust—even if it's broken.
- Use appreciation as a future-based tool for getting the best out of the player.
- Harness the full power of your listening—quite probably the most powerful coaching tool at your disposal.
- Read between the lines, decode secret agendas or motives, and put hidden, below-the-surface com-

munications on the table—without unleashing World War III.

iCoach4 will cover how you (and your players) build a future with and for people, a future that is compelling and irresistible, a future they want to commit to, that inspires them, that lights them up and gives them life. Perhaps the biggest value-add of a coach is to serve as advocate of the client's commitments and future. Learn (and coach your players on) how to:
- Build alignment and focus among multiple stakeholders.
- Overcome the three enemies of vision—resistance, resignation and apathy—and be free of any baggage from the past by putting it back where it belongs—in the past.
- Stand in the accomplishment—rather than in the status quo, no matter how pressing.
- Call forth solid commitment by—paradoxically—allowing for doubts and reservations.
- Let go of obsolete habits, and build habits consistent with your future.

iCoach5 will be about strategy. How do you (and your players) make the future doable for people, identify and provide whatever is missing, and remove any barriers to success? Working with my strategy clients over three-plus decades, I have developed powerful tools. How to build the bridge between the future and the now and how to do something that I call 'reverse road map' for example. Where you plan backwards but I don't want to give it away yet, no spoilers here.

So many ideas never see the light of day. So many commitments fall short of being realized. Why? Because people don't have the tools for moving from possibility to feasibility. How can you coach bosses, colleagues or clients to make the future feasible? I have coached Fortune 500 companies and startups, governments and the military to meet bold business impera-

tives. In this path-breaking book, I will show you (and your players):
- How to position yourself (themselves) as the CEO's strategy guru who manages strategy as a dynamic, agile, people-centered process.
- The four most powerful questions you (they) must ask to produce a shared understanding among multiple stakeholders and achieve the holy grail of strategy: alignment.
- How to align on the key performance indicators that match the future and pull for the right actions in the present.
- How to minimize resistance and pushback to change, integrate people power, and maximize ownership of the strategy.
- The Reverse Roadmap—planning back from the future to the Now, and how to sustain the momentum by managing not only the strategy's results but also its energy.

iCoach 6 highlights that supreme virtue—the action. How do you (and your players) communicate in a way that people produce decisive actions, breakthroughs and results they choose? How can your player take an obstacle or something that goes wrong, and turn it into an opportunity? How do you turn a breakdown into a breakthrough? That is the holy grail that will make you and your clients unstoppable. That and much more would be part of the action. It is all about getting, as German-speakers would put it, the PS on the road. *iCoach6* will show you the best action tools I have developed over 35+ years:
- How to generate decisive action—simply by what comes out of your (and the player's) mouth.
- Cockpit®, the system for managing all your (and the player's) commitments and maximizing your (and their) impact, peace of mind and freedom.
- Breakdown to Breakthrough: How to turn adversity

into an ally, any obstacle into an opportunity.
- How to connect each action with the big picture of vision and strategy, and building visual displays that pull for the highest-leverage actions.
- How to manage not just your project's actions and results, but its energy dynamics through a system of Operating Levels.
- The 7 best questions to ask the player in a post-mortem to leverage projects, activities or milestones achieved.

Finally, the culmination of the series is *iCoach 7*: how to institutionalize and/or standardize the momentum: successes, best practices, rituals.
- How to build a succession plan and an empowerment structure that fosters self-reliance and ends dependency on any personality in the firm.
- How to work yourself out of any job and free yourself while ensuring that your assets stay with the organization.
- How to make sure that clients come back to you (or that they stay away if you want them to).
- The power of completion and leveraging learnings.
- How to build Coaching-In-Action as a lucrative, high-margin business with zero-based budgeting.

In sum, I have created a system of six levels. It starts with coaching the player on self-knowledge and self-determination—from slavery to freedom. It then empowers the player's relationships and trust. It goes into the player's vision and future. It goes into the strategy and feasibility of that future. It focuses on the player's actions, breakthroughs and results. And the final building bloc is sustainability.

The series holds most of what I have learned and developed during 35 years of successful (and at times, failed) coaching. I want to give it all away because I am, for the first time in my life, considering semi-retirement. Yes, I plan to work for decades to come (just don't tell my wife that). I am in this for the long haul since it is so much fun—and I feel that my life does not ultimately belong to me alone. Nobody made this point more eloquently than George Bernard Shaw more than a century ago:

> This is the true joy in life, the being used for a purpose recognized by yourself as a mighty one, the being a force of nature instead of a feverish, selfish little clod of ailments and grievances complaining that the world will not devote itself to making you happy.
>
> I am of the opinion that my life belongs to the whole community and as long as I live it is my privilege to do for it whatever I can.
>
> I want to be thoroughly used up when I die, for the harder I work the more I live. I rejoice in life for its own sake. Life is no "brief candle" to me. It is a sort of splendid torch which I have got a hold of for the moment, and I want to make it burn as brightly as possible before handing it on to future generations.[47]

At the same time, I want to make these coaching tools available to as many people as I possibly can, so that the methodology doesn't depend on me alone. My vision is that it be available to everybody, regardless of their background or budget. This system has given my clients and me so much success, power, peace of mind, freedom and life that it would be a crime to withhold the knowledge.

So I am giving it to you (yes, you have to pay a minimal amount, calculated to cover my costs; all my book revenues either are re-invested in getting the word out, or fund non-profit causes). And I wish you all the best—may these tools bring you success, clients, great experiences in the exploration of Coaching-In-Action.

FURTHER READINGS

Block, Peter. 2011. *Flawless Consulting: A Guide to Getting Your Expertise Used.* Hoboken NJ: Pfeiffer / Wiley (3rd ed.).

Brounstein, Marty. 2011. *Coaching and Mentoring for Dummies.* New York: For Dummies / Wiley.

Bungay Stanier, Michael. *The Coaching Habit: Say Less, Ask More, and Change the Way You Lead Forever.* Toronto: Box of Crayons Press.

Buber, Martin. 1937. *I and Thou.* Edinburgh: T. & T. Clark.

Shmaya, David. *15-Minute Coaching: A Quick & Dirty Method for Coaches and Managers to Get Clarity About Any Problem.* Seattle WA: eCoachingSuccess.

Drucker, Peter. 1999. "Managing Oneself," *Harvard Business Review*, March-April 1999. 65-74.

Erhard, Werner, Michael C. Jensen and Steve Zaffron. 2007. "Integrity: a Positive Model that Incorporates the Normative Phenomena of Morality, Ethics and Legality." Harvard NOM Working Paper No. 06-11.

Flaherty, James. 1999. *Coaching: Evoking Excellence in Others.* Boston: Butterworth-Heinemann.

Goldsmith, Marshall, Laurence S. Lyons and Sarah McArthur. 2012. Hoboken NJ: Pfeiffer / Wiley.

Groysberg, Boris and Michael Slind. 2012. "Leadership Is a Conversation," *Harvard Business Review*. June.

Hargrove, Robert. 2008. *Masterful Coaching.* Hoboken NJ: Pfeiffer / Wiley.

Hargrove, Robert and Michel Renaud. 2004. *Your Coach (in a Book): Mastering the Trickiest Leadership, Business and Car-*

eer Challenges You Will Ever Face. San Francisco: Jossey-Bass.

Kahneman, Daniel, Andrew M. Rosenfield, Linnea Gandhi and Tom Blaser. 2016. "Noise: How to Overcome the High, Hidden Costs of Inconsistent Decision-Making," *Harvard Business Review*, October.

Schein, Edgar H. and Peter A. Schein. 2018. *Humble Leadership: The Power of Relationships, Openness and Trust.* San Francisco: Berret-Koehler.

Simpson, Michael. 2014. *Unlocking Potential: 7 Coaching Skills That Transform Individuals, Teams, and Organizations.* Seattle WA: Grand Harbor Press.

Solomon, Robert C. and Fernando Flores. 2001. *Building Trust: In Business, Politics, Relationships, and Life.* Oxford: Oxford University Press.

Stoltzfus, Tony. 2008. *Coaching Questions. A Coach's Guide to Powerful Asking Skills.* Redding CA: Coach22.

Sull, Donald N. and Charles Spinosa. 2007. "Promise-Based Management," Harvard Business Review, April.

Tichy, Noel M., Ram Charan and Lawrence A. Bossidy. 1995. The CEO As Coach: An Interview with AlliedSignal's Lawrence A. Bossidy. *Harvard Business Review*, April: 69-78.

Weber, Max. 1946, 1958. Bureaucracy. In H. H. Gerth and C. Wright Mills, eds. *From Max Weber: Essays in Sociology* (pp. 196-244). Oxford, England: Oxford University Press.

Wheatley, Margaret. 1996. *Leadership and the New Science.* San Francisco: Berret-Koehler.

Zweifel, Thomas D. 2003. *Communicate or Die: Getting Results Through Speaking and Listening.* New York: SelectBooks.

_____. 2013. *Culture Clash 2: Managing the Global High-Performance Team.* New York: SelectBooks.

_____. 2009. *Leadership in 100 Days: A Systematic Self-Coaching Workbook.* New York: iHorizon.

_____ and Edward J. Borey. 2014. *Strategy-In-Action: Marrying Planning, People and Performance.* New York: iHorizon.

_____ and Aaron L. Raskin. 2008. *The Rabbi & the CEO: The*

Ten Commandments for 21st-Century Managers. New York: SelectBooks.

THE AUTHOR

Dr. Thomas D. Zweifel is a strategy & performance expert, board member and sparring partner for CEOs & leaders of Fortune 500 companies. The ex-CEO of Swiss Consulting Group, named "Fast Company" by *Fast Company* magazine, has coached clients on four continents since 1984 to open strategic frontiers, meet business imperatives and seize growth opportunities. An authority on integrating planning, people and performance, Thomas helps clients ask the right questions, confront taboos, build strategy alignment, and boost productivity. Ultimately his specialty is unleashing the human spirit in organizations—without unnecessary blah-blah, impractical training programs, or false dependencies on high-priced consultants.

Selected corporate clients: ABB, Airbus, Banana Republic, Citibank, ConocoPhillips, Credit Suisse, Danone, Dell, Deutsche Bank, DHL, Faurecia, Fiat, GE, GM, Goldman Sachs, Google, J&J, JPMorgan Chase, Medtronic, Nestlé, Novartis, P&G, Prudential, Roche, Sanofi, Siemens, Starbucks, Swiss Re, UBS, Unilever, Zurich.

Selected other clients: Kazakhstan prime minister & cabinet, various Swiss government agencies, UNDP, US State Department, US Air Force Academy, US Military Academy West Point.

Board member: Paramount Business Jets, Keren Hayesod World Executive, International Journal of Communication Research.

Since 2001, Thomas has taught leadership at Columbia University and since 2004 at HSG (St. Gallen University). He is often featured in the media, including ABC, Bloomberg, CNN, Swiss National TV, *Fast Company* and *Financial Times*.

Thomas is the award-winning author of seven books on strategy and co-leadership, including *Communicate or Die: Getting Results Through Speaking and Listening* (SelectBooks 2003); *Culture Clash 2.0: Managing the Global High-Performance Team* (SelectBooks 2013); *Strategy-In-Action: Marrying Planning, People and Performance* (iHorizon 2014), a Readers Favorite Silver Award winner; and *The Rabbi and the CEO: The Ten Commandments for 21st Century Leaders* (SelectBooks 2008; with Aaron L. Raskin), a National Jewish Book Award finalist.

Born in Paris, Dr. Zweifel holds a Ph.D. in International Political Economy from New York University. In 1996 he realized his dream of breaking three hours in the New York City Marathon, and in 1997 was recognized as the "fastest CEO in the New York City Marathon." He lives in Zurich with his wife and two daughters.

OTHER BOOKS BY THOMAS D. ZWEIFEL

Communicate or Die: Getting Results Through Speaking and Listening (SelectBooks)

> "Everybody should read this book. You can substitute one evening of entertainment and make a difference in your life and work for years to come."
> **—Ali Velshi, Senior Economic and Business Correspondent, NBC**

Culture Clash 2.0: Managing the Global High-Performance Team (SelectBooks)

> "I just wish *Culture Clash* had been available at the start of my personal globalisation, it would have saved me a lot of time and pain. I would recommend this book as essential reading for any international manager."
> **—Dr. Martin Cross, CEO, Novartis-Australia**

Democratic Deficit? Institutions and Regulation in the European Union, Switzerland and the United States (Rowman Littlefield)

> "Thomas Zweifel's pathbreaking book delivers a compelling empirical analysis of transparency and accountability in the European Union. A must-read."
> **—Andrew Moravcsik, Professor, Princeton University and** *Newsweek*

International Organizations and Democracy: Accountability, Politics and Power (Lynne Rienner Publishers)

> "Zweifel's accessible book sets the stage for an informed debate on the place of 'We, The People' in global governance."
> **—Shepard Forman, Center on International Cooperation, New York University**

Leadership in 100 Days: Your Systematic Self-Coaching Roadmap to Power and Impact—and Your Future (iHorizon)

> "Very pragmatic self-study guide that with personal discipline provides a clear road map towards (increased) success."
> **—Hans Toggweiler, CEO Americas, DHL**

Strategy-In-Action: Marrying People, Planning and Performance (iHorizon; with Edward J. Borey) Silver Award, Business & Finance, Readers' Favorite

> "The only strategy book that gives a truly holistic view of strategy. It integrates strategy alignment, highly pragmatic execution and performance, and the human element in one seamless process."
> **—Dr. Frank Waltmann, Head of Learning, Novartis**

The Rabbi and the CEO: The Ten Commandments for 21st Century Leaders (SelectBooks; with Aaron L. Raskin) Finalist, National Jewish Book Award

> "The leadership wisdom contained here is timeless, powerful and actionable--just what you'd expect when you combine a Rabbi and a CEO!"
> **—Scott A. Snook, Professor of Organizational Behavior, Harvard Business School**

THOMASZ-WEIFEL.COM PROCESSES

If you are interested in harnessing Dr. Zweifel's methodologies for your organization, connect to www.ThomasZweifel.com for strategy and leadership processes, coaching and workshops that help leaders open strategic frontiers, meet business imperatives and/or cause performance breakthroughs.

> *Strategy-In-Action*: a 7-step process. Confidential and anonymous pre-interviews gather perspectives of all key stakeholders and lead to a shared understanding; a 2-day workshop aligns the management team around a bold business challenge and an elegant vision/strategy framework; and low-risk 100-Day pilots pull the future to the present, yield quick wins and provide feedback to the strategy.
>
> *Leadership-In-Action*: a 2-day workshop provides leadership tools that last; systematically develops your high-potential leaders and fills their leadership gaps; and challenges their leadership in the action of meeting breakthrough goals through 100-Day leadership projects.
>
> *Coaching-In-Action*: a 6-month process tailored to executives fosters breakthroughs in their leadership ability in the action of meeting a business and/or leadership challenge.
>
> *Communicate or Die*: a 2-day workshop gives leaders tools for effective speaking *and* masterful listening in teams and/or organizations.
>
> *Culture Clash*: a 2-day workshop prepares leaders to avoid costly mistakes when working with or in other cultures (e.g. in virtual teams and/or outsourcing), and get the job done while respecting local values and customs.

NOTES

[1] John P. Kotter, "Leading Witnesses," *Strategy and Business*, Summer 2004.

[2] Sharon Daloz Parks, 2005, *Leadership Can Be Taught*, Cambridge: Harvard Business School Press.

[3] Sharon Daloz Parks, "What Artists Know About Leadership," Harvard Business School Working Knowledge, 7 November 2005.

[4] Sharon Daloz Parks, 2005, *Leadership Can Be Taught*, Cambridge: Harvard Business School Press.

[5] Letter to Frederick William, Prince of Prussia, 28 November 1770.

[6] Herman J. Saatkamp Jr. and William G. Holzberger (eds.), *The Works of George Santayana* (ed.). Cambridge: MIT Press. 65.

[7] H.W. Brands, *Masters of Enterprise: Giants of American Business from John Jacob Astor and J.P. Morgan to Bill Gates and Oprah Winfrey*. New York: Free Press. 251.

[8] Abraham Joshua Heschel. 1997. "No Time for Neutrality," in *Moral Grandeur and Spiritual Audacity: Essays*. New York: Farrar Straus and Giroux. 101.

[9] Pirkei Avot 4:1b.

[10] *New York Times*, 5 August 2016.

[11] *ibid*.

[12] A few examples of the sports coaching literature for illustration only: B. Douge. 1993. "Coach Effectiveness," *Sport Science Review 2:2*, 14-29. B. Howe, 1993, "Psychological Skills and Coaching," *Sport Science Review 2:2*, 30-47. S.R. Pratt and D.S. Eitzen, 1989, "Contrasting Leadership Styles and Organizational Effectiveness: The Case of Athletic Teams," *Social Science Quarterly 70*, 311-322. A.C. Lacy, 1994, Analysis of Starter/Non-Starter Motor Skill Engagement and Coaching Behaviors in Collegiate Women's Volleyball, *Journal of Teaching in Physical Education 13:2*, 95-107.

[13] See, for example: C.K. Ferguson, 1986, "Ten Case Studies from an OD Practitioner's Experience: Coping with Organizational Conflict," *Organizational Development Journal, 4:4*, 20-30. D.T. Hall, K.L. Otazo and G.P. Hollenbeck, 1999, "Behind Closed Doors: What Really Happens in Executive Coaching," *Organ-

Dr. Thomas D. Zweifel

izational Dynamics, Winter, 39-53. P.J. Kelly, 1985, "Coach the Coach, *Training and Development Journal 39:11*, 54-55. R.R. Kilburg (Ed.), 1996, "Executive Coaching" [Special issue]. *Consulting Psychology Journal: Practice and Research 48:2*. H. Levinson, 1991, "Counseling with Top Management," *Consulting Psychology Bulletin 43:1*, 10-15. J.E. Lukaszewski, 1988, "Behind the Throne: How to Coach and Counsel Executives," *Training and Development Journal 42:10*, 32-35. J.J. O'Connell, 1990, "Process Consultation in a Content Field: Socrates in Strategy," *Consultation: An International Journal, 9:3*, 199-208. M. Popper and R. Lipshitz, 1992, "Coaching on Leadership," *Consultation: An International Journal, Leadership and Organization Development Journal, 13:7*, 15-18. L. Sperry, 1993, "Working with Executives: Consulting, Counseling, and Coaching," *Individual Psychology: Journal of Adlerian Theory, Research, and Practice, 49:2*, 257-266.

[14] G.E. Allenbaugh, 1983, "Coaching: A Management Tool for a More Effective Work Performance," *Management Review 72*, 21-26. S. Aurelio and J.K. Kennedy Jr., 1991, "Performance Coaching: A Key to Effectiveness," *Supervisory Management 36*, 1-2. A. Barratt, 1985, "Management Development: The Next Decade," *Journal of Management Development 4:2*, 3-9. C.R. Bell, 1987, "Coaching for High Performance," *Advanced Management Journal 52*, 26-29. G.A. Bielous, 1994, "Effective Coaching: Improving Marginal Performers," *Supervision 55*, 3-5. T.L. Brown, 1990, "Boss or Coach? It's Not What Works for You – It's What Works for Your Team," *Industry Week 239:8*, 4. P. Chiaramonte, 1993, "Coaching for High Performance," *Business Quarterly 58*, 1-7. S.L. Cohen and L. Cabot, 1982, "Managing Human Performance for Productivity," *Training and Development Journal 36:12*, 94-100. S. Cunningham, 1991, "Coaching Today's Executive," *Public Utilities Fortnightly 128*, 22-25. R.D. Evered and J.C. Selman, 1989, "Coaching and the Art of Management," *Organizational Dynamics 18*, 16-32. D.J. Good, 1993, "Coaching Practice in the Business-to-Business Environment," *Journal of Business and Industrial Marketing 8:2*, 53-60. K. Herring, 1989, "Coaches for the Bottom Line," *Personnel Administrator 34*, 22. G.K. Himes, 1984, "Coaching: Turning a Group Into a Team," *Supervision 46*, 14-16. G. Keeys, 1994, "Effective Leaders Need to be Good Coaches," *Personnel Management 26*, 52-54. W. Kiechel III, 1991, "The Boss as Coach," *Fortune 201*, 201. J.T. Knippen, 1990, "Coaching," *Management Accounting 71*, 36-38. A.B. Leibowitz, B. Kaye and C. Farren, 1986, "Overcoming Management Resistance to Career Development Programs," *Training and Development Journal 40:10*, 77-81. R.W. Lucas, 1994, "Performance Coaching Now and for the Future," *HR Focus 71*, 13. W.C. Miller, 1984, "The Value of Non-supervisory Feedback in Coaching Sessions," *Supervisory Management 29*, 2-8. C.D. Orth, H.E. Wilkinson and R.C. Benfari, 1987, "The Manager's Role as Coach and Mentor," *Organizational Dynamics 15:4*, 66-74. K.L. Rancourt, 1995, "Real-Time Coaching Boosts Performance," *Training and Development 49*, April, 53-56. L.M. Shore, 1986, "Developing Employees Through Coaching and Career Management," *Personnel 63*, 34-38. S.J. Stowell, 1988, "Coaching: a Commitment to Leadership," *Training and Development Journal 42*, June, 34-38. L.Tyson, 1983, "Coaching: A Tool for Success," *Training and Development Journal 37*, 30. E.J. Wallach, 1983, "Performance Coaching: Hitting the Bull's-Eye," *Supervisory Management 28*, November, 19-22. M.F. Wolff, 1993, "Become a Better Coach," *Research Technology*

Management 36, 10-11. Woodlands Group, 1980, "Management Development Roles: Coach, Sponsor, and Mentor," *Personnel Journal 59:11*, 918-921.

[15] D. Deepose, 1995, *The Team Coach*. New York: Amacom. K.A. Ericsson (Ed.), 1996, *The Road to Excellence: The Acquisition of Expert Performance in the Arts and Sciences, Sports and Games*. Mahwah NJ: Erlbaum. J.W. Gilley and N.W. Boughton, 1996, *Stop Managing, Start Coaching! How Performance Coaching Can Enhance Commitment and Improve Productivity.* New York: McGraw-Hill. R. Hargrove, 1995, *Masterful Coaching: Extraordinary Results by Impacting People and the Way They Think and Work Together*. Johannesburg, South Africa: Pfeiffer. I. Martin, 1996, *From Couch to Corporation: Becoming a Successful Corporate Therapist*. New York: John Wiley & Sons. J.C. Maxwell, 1995, *Developing the Leaders Around You*. Nashville TN: Nelson. JB. Miller and P.B. Brown, 1993, *The Corporate Coach*. New York: Harper Business. M. Minor, 1995, *Coaching for Development: Skills for Managers and Team Leaders*. Menlo Park CA: Crisp Publications. D.B. Peterson and M.D. Hicks, 1996, *The Leader as Coach: Strategies for Coaching and Developing Others*. Minneapolis MN: Personnel Decisions. J. Robinson, 1996, *Coach to Coach: Business Lessons from the Locker Room*. Johannesburg, South Africa: Pfeiffer. D. Shula and K. Blanchard, 1995, *Everyone's Coach*. New York: Harper Business. T. Voss, 1997, *Sharpen Your Team's Skills in Coaching*. New York: McGraw-Hill. J. Whitmore, 1994, *Coaching for Performance*. San Diego CA: Pfeiffer. R. Witherspoon and R.P. White, 1997, *Four Essential Ways that Coaching Can Help Executives*. Greensboro NC: Center for Creative Leadership.

[16] D.B. Peterson, 1993, "Skill Learning and Behavior Change in an Individually Tailored Management Coaching and Training Program," Doctoral dissertation, University of Minnesota. Thompson, 1987, "A Formative Evaluation of an Individualized Coaching Program for Business Managers and Professionals," Doctoral dissertation, University of Minnesota. D.J. Miller, 1990, "The Effect of Managerial Coaching on Transfer of Training," Doctoral dissertation, United States International University. M.P. Sawczuk, 1991, "Transfer-of-Training: Reported Perceptions of Participants in a Coaching Study in Six Organizations," Doctoral dissertation, University of Minnesota. S. Graham, J.F. Wedman, and B. Garvin-Kester, 1993, "Manager Coaching Skills: Development and Application," *Performance Improvement Quarterly* 6:1, 2-13. S. Acosta-Amad, 1992, "Training for Impact: Improving the Quality of Staff's Performance," *Performance Improvement Quarterly* 5:2, 2-12. P.J. Decker, 1982, "The Enhancement of Behavior Modeling Training of Supervisory Skills by the Inclusion of Retention Processes," *Personnel Psychology* 35:2, 323-332. See Kilburg, *Executive Coaching*, 56-59, for an excellent literature review.

[17] Jim Collins, 2001, *Good to Great*. New York: HarperBusiness, 130-133.

[18] Jonathan Sacks, 2018, *Pesach: Finding Freedom*. Jerusalem: Koren Publishers Jerusalem Ltd. 188.

[19] "Le doute n'est past une condition agréable, mais la certitude est absurde." Letter to Frederick II of Prussia, 6 April 1767.

[20] "Knicks' Resilience Gets a New Test," *New York Times*, 29 May 2000.

[21] Gary Hamel and C.K. Prahalad, 1989, "Strategic Intent," *Harvard Business*

Dr. Thomas D. Zweifel

Review.

[22] Mick Crews, remarks, conference call, 10 February 2004.

[23] Mick Crews, remarks, conference call, 10 February 2004.

[24] Atul Gawande, "Personal Best: Top Athletes and Singers Have Coaches. Should You?" *The New Yorker*, 3 October 2011.

[25] Atul Gawande, "Personal Best: Top athletes and singers have coaches. Should you?" *New Yorker*, 3 October 2011.

[26] Rosemary Azzaro, "Executive Coaching: Can It Help You Break Through?" *Skills for Success: HBA Bulletin*, May/June 1999.

[27] Peter Block, „Flawless Consulting" workshop, 2011.

[28] *New York Times* 22 June 2003. Section 8,1.

[29] Jill Hecht Maxwell and Michael Hopkins, "Who Do You Call When No One Has the Answers?" *The Inc Life*. 38-48.

[30] Marshall Goldsmith and Howard Morgan, "My Coach and I," *strategy + business*, Summer 2003.

[31] Marshall Goldsmith and Howard Morgan, "Leadership Is a Contact Sport: The 'Follow-Up Factor' in Management Development," *strategy + business*, December 2004.

[32] *Houston Chronicle*, 1 February 2002.

[33] Harari, Yuval Noah. 2016. *Sapiens: A Brief History of Humankind*. New York: HarperCollins. 28-29.

[34] Prahalad, C.K. and Gary Hamel. 1990. The Core Competence of the Corporation. *Harvard Business Review*, May-June 1990, 79-91.

[35] Wheatley, Margaret. *Leadership and the New Science*. San Francisco: Barrett-Köhler. 91.

[36] Simons and Chabris, Selective Attention Test, 1999. www.theinvisiblegorilla.com or https://www.youtube.com/watch?v=vJG698U2Mvo.

[37] Jennifer Allen, "'Best Wishes, George Allen's Daughter,'" *The New York Times Magazine*, 24 September 2000. 64-69.

[38] Jerry Seinfeld, 2002, "Comedian," documentary.

[39] I owe this story to my client and friend Judd Maltin at Dell.

[40] David Rock, 2006, "A Brain-Based Approach to Coaching," based on an interview with Jeffrey Schwartz, *International Journal of Coaching in Organizations*, 4(2), 32-43.

[41] Ibid.

[42] Michael Bungay Stanier, *The Coaching Habit: Say Less, Ask More, and Change*

the Way You Lead Forever. Toronto: Box of Crayons Press. 76.

[43] Meredith Levine, "Tell the Doctor All Your Problems, But Keep It to Less Than a Minute," *New York Times*, June 1, 2004.

Benedict Carey, "New Therapy On Depression Finds Phone Is Effective," *New York Times*, August 25, 2004.

[44] Ibid.

[45] Lawrence Dyche and Deborah Swiderski, "The Effect of Physician Solicitation Approaches on Ability to Identify Patient Concerns," *Journal of General Internal Medicine*, 20: 3, March 2005: 267–270.

[46] Roger D. Evered and James C. Selman, "Coaching and the Art of Management," *Organizational Dynamics* 18:2, Autumn 1989.

[47] George Bernard Shaw, *Man and Superman*, dedicatory letter.

Made in the USA
Columbia, SC
29 January 2020